THE TRUE CRIME LOVER'S GUIDE TO
LONDON

THE TRUE CRIME LOVER'S GUIDE TO LONDON

CHARLOTTE BOOTH

&

BRIAN BILLINGTON

White Owl
AN IMPRINT OF PEN & SWORD BOOKS LTD.
YORKSHIRE – PHILADELPHIA

First published in Great Britain in 2024 by
White Owl
An imprint of
Pen & Sword Books Ltd.
Yorkshire - Philadelphia

Copyright © Charlotte Booth and Brian Billington, 2024

ISBN 978 1 39903 126 4

The right of Charlotte Booth and Brian Billington to be identified as authors of this work has been asserted by them in accordance with the Copyright, Designs and Patents Act 1988.

A CIP catalogue record for this book is available from the British Library.

All rights reserved. No part of this book may be reproduced or transmitted in any form or by any means, electronic or mechanical including photocopying, recording or by any information storage and retrieval system, without permission from the Publisher in writing.

Printed and bound by Printworks Global Ltd, London/Hong Kong.
Design: SJmagic DESIGN SERVICES, India.

Pen & Sword Books Ltd. incorporates the imprints of Pen & Sword Books: After the Battle, Archaeology, Atlas, Aviation, Battleground, Discovery, Family History, History, Maritime, Military, Naval, Politics, Railways, Select, Transport, True Crime, Fiction, Frontline Books, Leo Cooper, Praetorian Press, Seaforth Publishing, Wharncliffe and White Owl.

For a complete list of Pen & Sword titles please contact

PEN & SWORD BOOKS LIMITED
George House, Units 12 & 13, Beevor Street, Off Pontefract Road, Barnsley, South Yorkshire, S71 1HN, England
E-mail: enquiries@pen-and-sword.co.uk
Website: www.pen-and-sword.co.uk

or

PEN AND SWORD BOOKS
1950 Lawrence Rd, Havertown, PA 19083, USA
E-mail: uspen-and-sword@casematepublishers.com
Website: www.penandswordbooks.com

CONTENTS

ILLUSTRATIONS 7
INTRODUCTION 10
HOW TO USE THIS BOOK 12

CHAPTER 1
TREASON 13

CHAPTER 2
SMUGGLING 17

CHAPTER 3
HIGHWAY ROBBERY 19

CHAPTER 4
PROSTITUTION 21

CHAPTER 5
THEFT 26

CHAPTER 6
BODY SNATCHERS 54

CHAPTER 7
MURDER 56

CHAPTER 8
SERIAL KILLERS 98

CHAPTER 9
MISCELLANEOUS CRIMES 136

CHAPTER 10
RELATED SITES 140
   EXECUTION SITES 140
   PRISONS 149
   POLICE STATIONS 152
   MUSEUMS 156

CHAPTER 11
SPECIALIST TOURS 157
   CHURCH TOUR 160
   CEMETERY TOUR 162
   PUB CRAWL 168
   MURDER LOCATIONS TOUR 176

REFERENCES 189

INDEX 190

ILLUSTRATIONS

All photographs were taken by the authors unless specified otherwise.

1. Westminster Hall, 3 St Margaret Street, SW1P 3JX
2. 1a Cato Street, W1H 5HG
3. 61 Harrington Gardens, SW7 4JZ
4. The Marquis, (was The Hole in the Wall) 51-52 Chandos Place, WC2N 4HS
5. St Paul's Church, Bedford Street, WC2E 9ED
6. Burlington Arcade, 51 Piccadilly, W1J 0QJ
7. 15 South Street, W1K 2XB
8. Hilton, 22 Park Lane, W1K 1BE
9. 58 Eardley Crescent, SW5 9JZ
10. Westminster Abbey, 20 Deans Yard, SW1P 3PA
11. St Margaret's Church, St Margaret Street, SW1P 3JX
12. Harrods, 87-135 Brompton Road, SW1X 7XL (courtesy of Mikegr on Wikicommons Media)
13. Liberty, Regent Street, Carnaby, W1B 5AH
14. Cartier, 40-41 Old Bond Street, W1S 4QR
15. Catchpole and Williams, 510 Oxford Street, W1K 7JA
16. The White House, 51 New Bond Street, W1S 1BJ
17. Elkington's, 22 Regent Street St James's, W1B 5RL
18. Harvey Nichols, 109-125 Knightsbridge, SW1X 7RJ
19. Debenhams, 27-37 Wigmore Street, W1U 1PN
20. Selfridges, 400 Oxford Street, W1A 1AB
21. Fortnum and Mason, 181 Piccadilly, St James's, W1A 1ER
22. Embassy Club, 7 Old Bond Street, W1S 4PN
23. Eastcastle Street, W1T 3QP
24. Bow Street Police Station, 4 Bow Street, WC2E 7AT
25. 41 Burlington Arcade, 51 Piccadilly, W1J 0QJ
26. Lloyd's Bank, 185 Baker Street, NW1 6XB
27. Le Sac, 189 Baker Street, NW1 6UY
28. Royal National Hotel, 38-51 Bedford Way, WC1H 0DG
29. Paris Jewels (was Hatton Garden Safety Deposit Ltd), 88-90 Hatton Garden, EC1N 8PN
30. Madison, 25 Hatton Garden, EC1N 8BQ
31. Tyburn (Marble Arch), W1C 1LX
32. Leicester Square, WC2H 7LU
33. St George-in-the-East Church, 14 Cannon Street Road, E1 0BH
34. Crown and Dolphin Pub, 56 Cannon Street Road, E1 0BL
35. Guy's Hospital, SE1 9GU
36. Sheen's Burial Ground, 52-58 Commercial Road and 109-153 Back Church Lane, E1 1LP

37. (Hen & Chickens) 54 Borough High Street, SE1 1XL
38. 215 Whitechapel Road, E1 1DE
39. 3 Sidney Square, Mile End Road, E1 2EY
40. Old Castle Street (was Castle Alley), Whitechapel, E6 1PP
41. 31 Turner Street, E1 2AS
42. London Hospital, Whitechapel Road, E1 1FR
43. Wizards and Wonders (was Lyons Corner House), 13 Coventry Street (corner of Rupert Street), W1D 7AG
44. Grand Hotel, Northumberland Avenue, WC2N 5BY
45. 21 & 27 Wardour Street, W1D 6PN
46. Savoy, Strand, WC2R 0EZ
47. Caxton Hall, 8-10 Caxton Street, SW1H 0AQ
48. 71a Elsham Road, West Kensington, W14 8HD
49. Wandsworth Prison, Heathfield Road, SW18 3HU (courtesy of geography.org.uk on Wikicommons Media)
50. Blue Lagoon, 50 Carnaby Street, W1F 9QF
51. Nag's Head, 53 Kinnerton Street, Knightsbridge, SW1X 8ED
52. J.S. Jays Jewellers, 73-75 Charlotte Street, W1T 4PL
53. The Little Club, 37 Brompton Road, SW3 1DE
54. Carroll's Club, 58 Duke Street, Mayfair, W1K 6JW
55. 23 Cecil Court, WC2N 4EZ
56. Blind Beggar Pub, 337 Whitechapel Road, E1 1BU
57. Tate Modern, Bankside, SE1 9TG
58. Shepherd's Bush Police Station, 252 Uxbridge Road, W12 7JA
59. Marylebone Magistrates' Court, 181 Marylebone Road, NW1 5BR
60. 59 Braybrook Street, W12 0AS
61. Braybrook Street Memorial
62. Parish Church of St Stephen and St Thomas, 1 Coverdale Road, W12 8JJ
63. 46 Lower Belgrave Street, SW1W 0LN
64. Plumbers Arms, 14 Lower Belgrave Street, SW1W 0LN
65. 5 Eaton Row, SW1W 0JA
66. 72a Elizabeth Street, SW1W 9PD
67. Clermont Club, 44 Berkeley Square, W1J 5AR
68. 51 Chester Square, SW1W 9EA
69. 1 Brick Lane, E1 7SA
70. Ye Frying Pan Pub, 16 Brick Lane, E1 6PU
71. Working Lad's Institute, 283 Whitechapel Road, E1 1BY
72. 35 Dorset Street, W1U 6QR
73. Queen's Head Pub, 74 Commercial Street, E1 6LY
74. Ten Bells Pub, 84 Commercial Street, E1 6QQ
75. Lilian Knowles House (was Providence Row Refuge), 50 Crispin Street, E1 6HQ
76. Happy Days Chip Shop, 44/46 Goulston Street, E1 7TP
77. Culpeper Pub (was Princess Alice), 40 Commercial Street, E1 6TB
78. 8 Whites Row (was Spitalfields Chambers), E1 7NF
79. Northumberland Arms Pub, 119 Tottenham Court Road, W1T 5AW

80. 369 Brixton Road, SW9 7DE
81. 60 Uxbridge Road, Shepherd's Bush, W12 8LP
82. Brixton Prison, Jebb Avenue, Brixton Hill, SW2 5XF (courtesy of David Anstiss on Wikimedia Commons)
83. 3-4 Archer Street, Piccadilly, W1D 7AP
84. 76 Gloucester Place, W1U 6DQ
85. Maison Lyons Corner House, 1 Marble Arch, W1H 7DX
86. 29 Southwick Street, nr Sussex Gardens, Tyburnia, W2 1JQ
87. 9/10 Gosfield Street, W1W 6HD
88. 187 Sussex Gardens, Tyburnia, W2 2RH
89. Onslow Court Hotel (The Kensington Hotel) 113 Queen's Gate, SW7 3LE
90. 79 Gloucester Road, SW7 5BW
91. Old Bailey, EC4M 7EH (Courtesy of GrindtXX on Wikimedia Commons)
92. Sindercombe Social (was Shepherd's Bush Hotel) 2 Goldhawk Road, W12 8QD
93. The 40 Elephants Cocktail Bar, 3-5 Great Scotland Yard, SW1A 2HN
94. The Globe Tavern, 8 Bedale Street, SE1 9AL
95. Statue of Queen Anne, St Paul's Churchyard, EC4M 8AD
96. St Giles-in-the-Fields Churchyard, St Giles High Street, WC2H 8LG
97. Tower of London, EC3N 4AB
98. Trinity Square Gardens, Tower Hill, EC3N 4DX (site of Tower Hill executions)

99. Lincoln's Inn Fields, WC2A 3BP
100. The Additional Ground in Drury Lane (Now Drury Lane Gardens), 57 Drury Lane, WC2B 5SN
101. Kennington Common, Kennington Park Road, SE11 4PP
102. 4 Whitehall Place, SW1A 2EG
103. Norman Shaw Buildings, Victoria Embankment, SW1A 2JH
104. New Scotland Yard, Victoria Embankment, SW1A 2JL
105. Smallest Police Station, Trafalgar Square, WC2N 5DN
106. Jack the Ripper Museum, 12 Cable Street, E1 8JJ
107. Masons Arms, (now The Portman) 51 Upper Berkeley Street, W1H 7QW
108. St Giles High Street, WC2H 8AB
109. Chingford Mount Cemetery, 121 Old Church Road, E4 6ST
110. East London Cemetery, Grange Road, E13 0HB
111. St Patrick's Roman Catholic Cemetery, Queen's Road, E17 8QP
112. Crossbones Cemetery, Union Street, SE1 1SD
113. Blind Beggar Pub (internal)
114. The Castle Farringdon, 34-35 Cowcross Street, EC1M 6DB
115. Punch Bowl Pub, 41 Farm Street, W1J 5RP
116. Goat Tavern, 3A Kensington High Street, W8 5NP
117. 86 Rochester Row, SW1P 1LJ
118. 13a Finborough Road, SW10 9DF
119. The Crown, 213 Borough High Street, SE1 1JA

INTRODUCTION

Researching and writing this book took us on a fascinating journey into the darker side of London history. One of the most intriguing aspects of this research was learning about what went on behind the doors of unremarkable houses, to unremarkable people who then found themselves in remarkable circumstances. For example, we have included the pubs that murder victims drank in, as well as the homes they lived in – places they lived their day-to-day lives without knowing what was around the corner for them. This led us to consider the layers and layers of history which each house, business and building holds in London, many of which are potentially lost to the historical record. It certainly made us look at the city in a new light.

Considered Choices

Another thing that we learnt along the way were the ethical considerations of a book of this type. Some people will consider a tour taking people to the houses where murders took place to be distasteful, and this is something we understand.

However, we thought about such considerations in the events we represented, and how they were presented. It is important to realise that history isn't a sanitised, happy place. For every achievement, and celebration there is a crime or the darker side of human nature. Censoring that dark side gives a skewed view of history which is something we did not want to do.

Therefore, whilst we made the decision to include sites of murders, we have a cut-off point of 1975, as beyond this we thought to be too recent and would be disrespectful to the families of the victims. This has therefore meant that some infamous murders such as those of Dennis Nilsen whose murders spanned from 1978-1983, or the murder of Alexander Litvinenko in 2006 have been omitted. Other crimes do extend past this cut-off of 1975 although in the complex Brink's-Mat Robbery (page 46) the various murders which happened in association with it and the aftermath have also been omitted.

This wasn't an easy decision to make, especially when there have been films, TV shows and documentaries about certain murders since 1975, but it didn't feel right to include them. Also, in an effort to counter some of the ethical issues associated with the sites of murders, where known, we have also included the burial sites and hope that visitors will visit the victims' final resting places and perhaps leave a flower or at least spare a thought for their final moments.

Redevelopment

Another particular problem we also came up against in the compilation of this book was the constant redevelopment of London. The further back in time the crime was committed the less likely there was of there being a building or structure to visit. Add to that, at certain points in history different parts of London were practically flattened and then rebuilt.

In the nineteenth century a lot of the East End slums were pulled down and redeveloped removing any sixteenth-, seventeenth- and eighteenth-century buildings and the Blitz in 1940-41 destroyed a lot of central London losing any Elizabethan and Tudor buildings which had survived the earlier Great Fire of London (1666). Even the cemeteries weren't safe and with the development of the suburban graveyards (e.g. Highgate, Kensal Rise, Abney Park) the majority of the earlier inner-city graveyards were dug up and the bodies removed before the sites were redeveloped into parks and public spaces. This sadly therefore removed many of the sites of the work of the body snatchers or resurrection men.

London is constantly being redeveloped and Tom Quinn blithely commented that; "far more of old London was destroyed and continued to be destroyed by developers than by the Luftwaffe." And this remains to be true. In recent years there has been large scale destruction caused by Crossrail removing many cemeteries as well as old buildings which had otherwise survived through centuries, as well as large redevelopment of the East End for the 2012 Olympics.

All of this redevelopment means the East End of Jack the Ripper no longer exists, the London of the Krays is unrecognisable and Tyburn is now Marble Arch whereas it originally stood in the middle of the country. It also means that not all of the stories within these pages are complete, as they have been told according to the sites which are still standing. This book is therefore not meant to be a history book, offering you everything you need to learn about a particular crime, and you may be inspired to read further into crimes you didn't know about, or feel that crimes you are familiar with are not covered in enough detail. We have let the sites and locations tell the story, and if the locations no longer exist some elements of the stories have been omitted.

HOW TO USE THIS BOOK

We thank you for choosing this book and deciding to take us on your visits to London. The first thing we should say is that this book is by no means a definitive guide to all the crimes that have ever been committed in London. That in itself would be an impossible task.

Instead it is a snapshot of a number of crimes spanning over the past 700 years or so. We have covered 65 crimes or groups of crimes in the case of serial killers or serial thieves. Considering that in London in 2022, nearly 836,000 crimes were reported (not committed but only reported) you can see this really is a snapshot. A snapshot of the notorious, ridiculous, brutal and recurring crimes which tell a dark history of London through the surviving buildings.

As people who have used city guidebooks before and have already written another in the series (*Movie Lover's Guide to London*) we have laid this book out in a way which makes sense to us, and hopefully will to you too.

You will first of all notice there are no maps in the book. Instead there are very precise postcodes meaning the locations will be easily located using your smartphone whilst in the city or will enable you to plan ahead and create a Google Maps route before you go.

This is a deliberate decision, because this book covers all areas of London, including as far as Wembley, Twickenham and Amersham. This would therefore require the equivalent of an A-Z to cover all the sites. With technology developing at the speed it is, we felt this would be redundant as most visitors would be using their maps app anyway.

The book is divided into three main sections: the crimes, crime-related sites and specialist tours. In the crime section you will find the sites laid out by specific crime type and then in date order rather than by area. This means if you are following the sites of a particular crime it will make more sense than organised by area. In many cases a lot of the locations of the crimes are all within a particular area and locations from a particular crime (i.e. Jack the Ripper) are all presented together.

The specialist tours are laid out in themes (cemeteries, pubs, churches and murder locations) meaning you can search for specific types of buildings. However, if you happen to find yourself in a particular area, you can find any nearby sites by using the postcode index, allowing you to put together your own tours based on your location for the day. We hope this means this book will be flexible and enable you to enjoy your visits to London more.

We hope you enjoy this book, see some beautiful buildings and learn something new about this fabulous city, even if it is the more sinister side of human nature.

1

TREASON

William FitzOzbert (1196)

St Mary-le-Bow Church, Cheapside, EC2V 6AU

William FitzOzbert or 'Longbeard' was known for challenging authority, and during a siege following his public denouncement of the throne he killed a Kingsman. In his panic he fled and sought sanctuary in St Mary-le-Bow church and hid with nine of his conspirators.

The King's Men went against protocol and started a fire in the grounds of the church in order to 'smoke' the conspirators out so they could be arrested.

Tyburn (Marble Arch), W1C 1LX

William FitzOzbert was then the first person sentenced to death at Tyburn on April 6, 1196.

He was dragged behind a horse for the five miles from the Tower of London before he was hanged. FitzOzbert was not only the first to be executed at Tyburn, but also the first to become a martyr.

The junction between Edgware Road and Oxford Street marks Tyburn which between 1196 and 1783 was used as a place of execution. At the time it was open country and was on the main route to Oxford, which is why Tyburn Road was renamed as Oxford Street.

William Wallace (1305)

Westminster Hall, 3 St Margaret Street, SW1P 3JX

William Wallace, the Scottish patriot, went on trial at Westminster Hall in 1305 for treason against the king and the 'people of England and Scotland'.

He was forced to wear a crown of laurels as a means of mocking him. He was sentenced to be hanged, drawn and quartered for 'robberies, homicides and felonies' and to be beheaded "as an outlaw ... and afterwards for your burning churches and relics your heart, liver, lungs and entrails from which your wicked thoughts come shall be burned."

Smithfield, Grand Avenue, EC1A 9PS

In 1305 William Wallace was executed here for treason.

The market which currently sits on the site was designed by Sir Horace Jones in the later nineteenth century.

Westminster Hall, 3 St Margaret Street, SW1P 3JX

Oliver Cromwell (1658)

Westminster Abbey, Dean's Yard, SW1P 3PA

Oliver Cromwell was buried in Westminster Abbey in 1658 and was given the equivalent of a state funeral which cost in the region of £60,000 at the time. However, in 1661 he had been posthumously tried for regicide for his role in the death of Charles I and found guilty. His body was dug up and placed in a gibbet which was hung outside the Abbey. His head was put onto a spike outside Westminster Hall and remained there for 20 years.

After that it was removed and displayed in numerous local pubs.

Wig and Pen, 229-230 Strand, Temple, WC2R 1BF

Oliver Cromwell's skull was displayed at the Wig and Pen Pub and was eventually treated to forensic tests which showed it to be genuine. The skull was returned to his Cambridge College and has since been reburied.

Cato Street Conspiracy (1820)

1a Cato Street, W1H 5HG

Following the death of George III in January 1820, Arthur Thistlewood and his fellow conspirators hatched a plan to use this time to unseat the current government by charging into the house

1a Cato Street, W1H 5HG

of Lord Harrowby, the Lord President of the Council, during a Cabinet Meeting and assassinate the entire cabinet in one go.

Their headquarters was a disused stable, which is now 1a Cato Street (with the black frontage). They accidently recruited a police spy into their gang as well as approaching a random cow-keeper, Thomas Hidon, who reported everything to Lord Harrowby leading to their capture.

On February 23, 1820, the Bow Street Runners charged the stable in order to arrest the gang. Thistlewood murdered one officer, but the other conspirators were using low-quality gunpowder causing the guns to backfire. Thistlewood and three conspirators escaped but the others were arrested. Thistlewood was arrested a few days later. Eleven conspirators were charged and hanged for their part in the plot.

There is a blue plaque on the building commemorating that the conspiracy was uncovered at this site.

Old Bailey, EC4M 7EH
The conspirators were tried at the Old Bailey on March 23, 1820. They were found guilty of treason and sentenced to be hanged, drawn and quartered. This was carried out at Newgate Prison.

2

SMUGGLING

**The Gun Tavern, Docklands,
27 Coldharbour, E14 9NS**
www.thegundocklands.com

Within this pub there is an enclosed staircase which has a smugglers' spy hole cut into the wall for those landing contraband on the dock and distributing it via a hidden tunnel. This was used as a means to evade the revenue officers.

This pub dates back to the early eighteenth century but took its current name from the cannon which was fired to celebrate the opening of the West India Import Docks in 1802.

This pub was also used by Lord Horatio Nelson to meet Emma Hamilton in what is now the River Room. There is also a rumour that there was a tunnel between the pub and her lodgings in Cold Harbour. In the late eighteenth century, Nelson acquired a property just up the road (still known as Nelson's House).

Berry Bros. & Rudd, 3 St James's Street, SW1A 1EG
In the 1920s, an American, Jack 'Legs' Diamond, walked into Berry Bros & Rudd and ordered several hundred cases of whisky. In itself not a crime,

except that at the time America was in the middle of prohibition.

Evidence shows that Berry Bros. & Rudd delivered a large order of Cutty Sark whisky to the Bahamas, at the time a British colony. It is thought that from there it was smuggled into the US at the New Jersey coast.

This seemed to be a common 'crime' as in 1918, before prohibition the Bahamas drank 944 gallons of whisky. This rose by 1922 to 386,000 gallons a year! Although the US government raised the issue of British imports to the Caribbean there was nothing that could be done as it was all legal and above board.

Berry Bros. & Rudd opened in 1698 and sells more than 5,000 wines selected by five Masters of Wine, with two royal warrants.

Noreen Harbord (1946)

61 Harrington Gardens, SW7 4JZ
Noreen Harbord, Queen of the Contraband Coast, lived here in 1939. She had married Arthur Harold Harvard, son of a brigadier in 1936 but by the time she lived here in 1946 they were separated.

She led ships smuggling contraband goods like cigarettes, nylons, alcohol or penicillin into the UK at a time when rationing was still in place. She then moved onto gold strips, and finally Swiss watches in 1949.

She was an ex-debutante and society hostess and at 18 had been presented at Buckingham Palace.

61 Harrington Gardens, SW7 4JZ

HIGHWAY ROBBERY

Shooters Hill, SE18 4LG
Shooters Hill was once lined with woodland making a perfect location for highwaymen. If they were captured and executed their bodies were often hung in gibbets along the road as a deterrent. Samuel Pepys, writing in 1661, said:

> "Mrs Anne and I rose under the man that hangs upon Shooters Hill and a filthy site it was to see how his flesh had shrunk to his bones."

This is hard to imagine when looking up this leafy suburban street.

Wimbledon Common, SW15 3SB
In 1795 the body of hanged highwayman, Lewis Avershaw/Abershaw was displayed on Wimbledon Common, on the place known as Jerry's Hill. The Sunday after it was gibbeted, London was empty as people flocked to see it. It was there for four months and was a big draw for tourists.

Claude Du Vall (1670)

The Marquis, (was The Hole in the Wall) 51-52 Chandos Place, WC2N 4HS
This pub dates back to 1765 and is thought by some to be on the site

The Marquis, (was The Hole in the Wall) 51-52 Chandos Place, WC2N 4HS

of the Hole in the Wall pub where notorious highwayman Claude Du Vall (Duvall/Duval) was arrested in 1670.

Tyburn (Marble Arch), W1C 1LX
On January 21, 1670 Du Vall was hanged at Tyburn.

St Paul's Church, Bedford Street, WC2E 9ED
Claude Du Vall was apparently buried in the Chancel at St Paul's, Covent Garden. As a popular celebrity his funeral was attended by thousands of women from the aristocracy to prostitutes. He was reported as never using violence and was a very popular romantic figure. On his gravestone there was an inscription which read:

"Here lies Duval: reader, if male thou art, Look to thy purse: if female to thy heart. Much havoc hath he made of both: for all. Men made me stand, and women made me fall. The second conqueror of the Norman Race, Knights to his arms die yield, and ladies to his face. Old Tyburn's Glory, England's bravest thief: Duval the ladies joy, Duval the ladies grief."

St Paul's Church, Bedford Street, WC2E 9ED

PROSTITUTION

In the nineteenth century prostitution was vilified, meaning sex workers were criminalised as were their patrons. However in earlier centuries prostitution was accepted to a certain extent as a legitimate occupation.

In the twelfth century for example, the Bishop of Winchester and the church made a lot of money from prostitution, and in Southwark prostitutes were known as Bishop of Winchester's Geese.

Despite this, they were unable to be buried in consecrated land, and were considered lower class citizens. The only exception to this were high class prostitutes or concubines and mistresses who slept with kings and princes.

Burlington Arcade, 51 Piccadilly, W1J 0QJ

In the nineteenth century, prostitutes rented many of the rooms above the shops in the Burlington Arcade. They had a great view of the entire arcade, and when they saw a beadle they whistled a warning to the pickpockets below. It was at this time that whistling was banned in the arcade and is a rule upheld today by the beadles who are still policing the area. Only two people have permission to whistle in the arcade: Paul McCartney and a young lad

Burlington Arcade, 51 Piccadilly, W1J 0QJ

called Jaden from the East End who was given dispensation by the beadles.

The beadles are a private security force introduced by Lord George Cavendish, owner of Burlington House on Piccadilly, and were originally pulled from the 10th Hussars. He built the arcade in

1819 to protect his property from oyster shells being lobbed over his garden wall (the equivalent of McD wrappers).

Crossbones Cemetery, Union Street, SE1 1SD
www.crossbones.org.uk

Between the sixteenth century and 1853, this unconsecrated burial ground was used "for the interment of the low women who frequented the neighbourhood" and then for the paupers and those who were forbidden to be buried in a churchyard.

There were so many burials here that in the 1850s the bodies were buried close enough to the surface, that hands and feet were often seen poking through the sod.

It was closed as a burial ground in 1853 due to the overcrowding and the land sold in 1883 as a building site.

In the 1920s, during building work forty bodies were uncovered and reburied in Brockwood Cemetery in Woking. In the 1990s and the extension of the Jubilee Line, 148 further bodies were uncovered. In 2014 it was set up as a memorial garden.

Catherine Walters (1860s)

15 South Street, W1K 2XB
This was the home of Catherine Walters, who was nicknamed 'Skittles' as she had once worked in a bowling alley. She has been lauded as one of the 'last great

15 South Street, W1K 2XB

courtesans of London.' Amongst her 'clients' were rumoured to be Edward VII, Napoleon III and William Gladstone.

She received enough money from Lord Hartington whom she called 'Harty Tarty' to rent this house in Mayfair. He caused a society scandal by openly escorting Catherine to the Epsom Derby.

She was able to purchase the house in 1872 when she returned some love letters to Bertie, Prince of Wales (later

Edward VII) who gave her a lot of money in gratitude. She lived here until her death in 1920 leaving everything to her lover, Gerald Le Marchant Saumerez who was 21 years her junior.

In 2021 the house was rented for the sum of £5,000 per week. There is a blue plaque on the building commemorating her time here.

Miss Whiplash (1980s)

(Odeon and Empire Cinemas), Leicester Square, WC2H 7LU
Before Lindi St Clair (aka Miss Whiplash), became a high-class prostitute and dominatrix, she worked as an usher at the Odeon and a booking agent at the Empire cinema. She used these jobs as 'alibis' when she was walking though Soho at night looking for 'punters'.

Sandringham Flats, 87 Charing Cross Road, WC2H 0BN
When Lindi was still working as a street prostitute, she took some clients to the flat roof on Sandringham Flats which provided a covered spot as well as fire escapes should a quick exit be required.

Ace Corner, North Circular Road, NW10 7UD
In the 1970s, when she was turning tricks she spent time with the Hell's Angels and was known as Lady Scratch. She was interviewed at this café by a reporter from *The Observer*.

39 Curzon Street, W1J 7TZ
In the 1970s there was an open brothel at this address that had a neon sign in the window which said, "French Lessons". Through the front window there were two leather high-back chairs placed opposite each other, one with the back to the window. The prostitutes sat in the other chair in full view of the street.

London Hotels
When Lindi opened her first brothel she solicited in these hotels whilst on drinking binges with her friends: She was once arrested outside the Hilton where she was cautioned and released.
- Regent Palace Hotel, 36 Glasshouse Street, W1B 5DL
- The Cumberland Hotel, 1 Great Cumberland Place, W1H 7DL
- Hilton Hotel, 22 Park Lane, W1K 1BE

Savoy, Strand, WC2R 0EZ
When Lindi returned to London after working in a Paris brothel she booked a suite at the Savoy. She stayed here whilst she found the perfect property for her own brothel.

58 Eardley Crescent, SW5 9JZ
Lindi decided on 58 Eardley Crescent which had a basement that was turned into a dungeon. Here she ran her House of Fetish and Fantasy and where she entertained her clients, which included MPs, judges and lawyers. She also rented a house a few doors down, and some

24 | THE TRUE CRIME LOVER'S GUIDE TO LONDON

Hilton, 22 Park Lane, W1K 1BE

PROSTITUTION | 25

58 Eardley Crescent, SW5 9JZ

of her VIP clients entered this flat and headed over to number 58 via the roof.

Thai Square at Wig and Pen, 229-230 Strand, WC2R 1BF

When Lindi was on trial at the law courts opposite the Wig and Pen pub, she received messages from her clients asking to meet her here afterwards. She was being sued by Inland Revenue for non-payment of tax, even though she was unable to register her business as prostitution is illegal. She lost the case.

5
THEFT

Westminster Abbey Robbery (1303)

Westminster Abbey, 20 Deans Yard, SW1P 3PA

In 1303, the apparently impregnable royal treasury at Westminster Abbey was robbed, losing the amount of £100,000 (£20m in modern currency). Royal regalia, silver plate, coins and jewellery were stolen as well as the funds Edward I was planning to use for his ongoing war in Scotland.

The monks had, a few months before the robbery, planted a plot of hemp in the cemetery cloisters where the gains were stashed before being removed by monk Alexander of Pershore.

The robbery had been planned by William the Sacrist, the churchwarden and Richard de Podlicote, the keeper of the Palace of Westminster and their servants.

St Margaret's Church, St Margaret Street, SW1P 3JX
www.westminster-abbey.org/st-margarets-church

In 1863, the doors from St Margaret's Church leading to the treasury were thought to be covered in human skin and it was rumoured that these were the remains of William the Sacrist.

Today the Abbey claim the skin is cowhide. Even so, the door is Britain's oldest and leads to the Chapter House.

Left: *Westminster Abbey, 20 Deans Yard, SW1P 3PA*

Opposite: *St Margaret's Church, St Margaret Street, SW1P 3JX*

Tower of London, EC3N 4AB
Once the robbery had been discovered at the treasury 41 friars and 34 monks were arrested and taken to the Tower of London. Ten monks and one cleric were arraigned but refused to be judged by secular judges.

The Forty Thieves (1890s-1950s)

118 Stamford Street, Blackfriars, SE1 9NN
Mary Carr was the first queen of the Forty Thieves (aka the Forty Elephants), a group of women who excelled in extortion, theft, shoplifting and blackmail.

In 1893, she was living here with her husband, Alf Garmen, the leader of the Elephant and Castle gang. It was at this time she left Garmen to travel to Antwerp in order to sell a stolen diamond.

This address was also the site of the murders of Alice Marsh and Emma Shrivell by Thomas Cream in 1892.

Southwark Police Court, 211 Tooley Street, SE1 2JY
In spring 1896, Mary was arrested and charged here for the kidnapping of a six-year-old boy.

In 1905 this building was renamed Tower Bridge Police Court. It is now the Dixon Hotel.

Old Bailey, EC4M 7EH
Mary's trial was held here. She was charged with the kidnapping of 6-year-old Michael McGee who had been 'stolen from his mother' at Epsom. The police found he had been well looked after at the Stamford Street address.

Mary's defence was that Phil Jacobs had asked her to look after his son, which she did, although he stated

she had asked him to take the boy to Stamford Street.

She was found guilty and sentenced to three years in prison. Michael McGee was then sent to the Society of Suppression of Vice with his mother's consent after it was revealed he had contracted an STD whilst at Stamford Street.

Department Stores
- Harrods, 87-135 Brompton Road, SW1X 7XL
- Liberty, Regent Street, Carnaby Street, W1B 5AH
- Whiteley's, 149 Queensway, W2 4YN (This is currently being refurbished into luxury flats.)

Harrods, 87-135 Brompton Road, SW1X 7XL
Courtesy of Mikegr on Wikicommons Media

Liberty, Regent Street, Carnaby, W1B 5AH

Mary Carr and the Forty Thieves targeted all major department stores in London and shoplifted in groups. They were a well-trained team and went to these stores around tea time when they were busy. They all worked in teams of three; one to act as a block, another to steal and the third in the getaway car.

Murray's "Cabaret" Club, 16-18 Beak Street, W1F 9RD

The Forty Thieves often went to Murray's Cabaret Club in Beak Street in the late 1920s to dance the night away and spend some of the takings from selling their stolen goods.

This club closed in 1975.

43 Club, 43 Gerrard Street, W1D 5QQ

The Forty Thieves including Alice Diamond and Maggie Hughes, both subsequent leaders of the gang unwound here in the later 1920s.

The club opened in 1921, and was popular with nobility, members of Parliament, writers and the judiciary.

The club was raided in 1924 and 42 men and women were charged with after-hours drinking. It eventually closed to be re-opened as Proctors and then the Gerrard Club.

35 Johanna Street, SE1 7RG

On December 21, 1925 there was a riot in this small street which included the Forty Thieves, all focused on Marie Britten's house at number 35.

There had been a dispute between two members of the gang, Marie Britten and Bertha Tappenden, at the Canterbury Social Club, New Cut on December 19. Bertha was injured when Marie's father threw a glass of stout at her, and Marie bit her finger.

This then escalated and after getting fuelled up in the Canterbury Social Club a gang led by Alice Diamond and Gert Scully, all armed with bottles went to deal with Marie Britten on Johanna Street.

Everyone within Marie's house was injured as the crowd surged in. Marie hid her new-born baby under the bed. When the police arrived they were also attacked as they attempted to reach the house.

Old Bailey, EC4M 7EH

On March 18, 1926, Alice Diamond, Bertha Tappenden, Gertrude Scully and Maggie Hughes stood trial at the Old Bailey for their role in the riot.

Alice and Bertha were sentenced to 18-months with hard labour and Gertrude and Maggie were given 21-months.

Lilian Goldstein (aka the Bobbed-Hair Bandit) (1926-1940)

Cartier, 40-41 Old Bond Street, W1S 4QR

At 11am one morning in 1926, Lilian Goldstein drove her car onto the pavement in front of Cartier on Bond Street, blaring her horn and alarming the door man. She then rammed the front of her car into the door.

Charles Ruby Spark (aka Ruby Sparks or Sparkes) was in a car behind with another gangster. He did the same with his car before emerging through a hole he had cut in the roof of the car, smashed

Cartier, 40-41 Old Bond Street, W1S 4QR

*Catchpole and Williams,
510 Oxford Street, W1K 7JA*

Cartier's window and grabbed £18,000 (£1 million today) worth of jewellery.

Lilian in the meanwhile got out of her car and started making her way home. Her stylish bobbed haircut earned her the nickname the Bobbed-Hair Bandit.

Lilian and Ruby were the smash and grab Bonnie and Clyde with Lilian acting as a getaway driver and decoy. Over the years they committed numerous smash and grab robberies as well as regular house breaking.

Catchpole and Williams, 510 Oxford Street, W1K 7JA

Charles Spark's first attempt at smash-and-grab was in 1926 when he tried to rob the crown jewellers, Catchpole and Williams. He threw a brick at the window not realising it was reinforced glass and so it bounced off. He tried a few more times with the same result whilst drawing the amused attention of passers-by.

Today this store is a Superdrug.

The White House, 51 New Bond Street, W1S 1BJ

In July 1933, Lilian was convicted of stealing lingerie from this milliners on New Bond Street. She had hidden £104 worth of items underneath her clothes.

She pleaded guilty and received a sentence of four months hard labour. The police suspected her of being the Bobbed-Hair Bandit but there wasn't enough evidence.

Today the store is an Emporio Armani.

The White House, 51 New Bond Street, W1S 1BJ

Elkington's, 22 Regent Street, St James's, W1B 5RL

On February 8, 1930, a gang of burglars, climbed through the back of Elkington's on Regent Street where they were undergoing building works, smashed a window and stole £250 worth of jewellery. This was one of four raids carried out that evening.

Today this building is a Vispring Bed Store.

Elkington's, 22 Regent Street, St James's, W1B 5RL

58 Wembley Park Drive, HA9 8HB

On June 27, 1940, Lilian stopped off at this address before heading to the Ritz Cinema to meet Ruby. Her husband Jim Duggan had rented this property from May 18, 1940.

Ritz Cinema, 277 Neasden Lane, NW10 1QJ

On June 27, 1940, Lilian met Ruby outside the cinema and had a brief conversation with him before he ran off. He had escaped from Dartmoor prison six months earlier and was on the run but due to their relationship Lilian had a 24-hour police watch on her leading to his arrest.

Today the façade of the cinema has been pulled down and houses the Christ Embassy, but you can see the original Art Deco decoration on the two adjacent buildings.

Willesden Police Station, 96 High Road, NW10 2PP

Ruby Spark was taken to Willesden Police Station, where he produced false identity before eventually admitting he was Charles Ruby Spark.

The building is currently empty but plans have been presented for a large residential redevelopment.

10 Richmond Court, Forty Avenue, Wembley, HA9 8LL

Lilian was arrested for harbouring an escaped prisoner in her Wembley home. She lived here with her husband Jim Duggan, who was a member of the Billy Hill Gang. She told police she had nothing to do with Ruby Spark and hadn't seen him, but when searching the house, they found clothes which connected her to him.

Old Bailey, EC4M 7EH

The trial started in mid-July, 1940 and Ruby was sentenced to a further twelve months in prison. Lilian was sentenced to six months but was recalled to court a week later and the sentence was changed to three years' probation as she "no doubt found it difficult to act otherwise in assisting this old lover of yours" said the judge and that she had "followed a very natural womanly instinct in trying to succour and protect this man with whom you had intimate relations over a period of years."

She was never convicted for any of the smash-and-grab raids she had participated in since the 1920s even though she had been arrested a number of times for theft. They were never able to link her to Ruby Spark's business.

Penguin Club, 27 Rupert Street, Soho, W1D 6DR

When Ruby got out of prison in 1944 he opened this club in Soho, but it was later closed for harbouring criminals.

Shirley Pitts (1950s)

Harvey Nichols, 109-125 Knightsbridge, SW1X 7RJ

In the late 1940s Shirley was taught to shoplift by Alice Diamond of the Forty Thieves which included going to Harvey Nichols. Shirley was impressed by the toilets here as it was the first time she had been to a public bathroom where you had your own marble sink with powder and a hairbrush for your personal use.

In one hoist here she boasted that she took three fur coats in one swoop and put them down her customised shoplifting bloomers. As she waddled out of the store, the floorwalker who was there to prevent shoplifting was worried she was about to give birth.

Debenhams, 27-37 Wigmore Street, W1U 1PN

The Forty Thieves also took the 13-year-old Shirley to Debenhams in Wigmore Street to practice shoplifting in 1947.

The Forty Thieves had targeted this store since the 1920s and on December 23, 1927 it was part of the great ghost raid, where 14 cars of thieves left the Elephant and Castle and headed to numerous department stores including Debenhams. How much stock was stolen was never

Harvey Nichols, 109-125 Knightsbridge, SW1X 7RJ

disclosed as the stores wanted to downplay the event.

This store opened in 1908 and closed in the 1980s.

Harrods, 87-135 Brompton Road, SW1X 7XL
In the 1960s whilst shoplifting in Harrods, Shirley had the audacity to remove a £15k fur coat from a mannequin and replace it with a mackintosh she had stolen from elsewhere.

Selfridges, 400 Oxford Street, W1A 1AB
From the 1950s through to the 1980s Shirley shoplifted from Selfridges. Often she shoplifted to order with a 24-hour turnaround. In the mid-70s however, she said her driver found it more difficult to park, and was often moved on by traffic wardens, making

Debenhams, 27-37 Wigmore Street, W1U 1PN

Selfridges, 400 Oxford Street, W1A 1AB

shoplifting and the subsequent getaway more difficult.

Fortnum and Mason, 181 Piccadilly, St James's, W1A 1ER

Another of Shirley's regular haunts was Fortnum and Mason where she stole a whole rail of clothes at a time and shoved them into a large bag. She focused on big names like Chanel, Christian Dior and Yves Saint Laurent. She often bought a few pieces, especially shoes as they were normally only displayed with one shoe, in order to complete an outfit.

Embassy Club, 7 Old Bond Street, W1S 4PN

One of Shirley's regular haunts was the Embassy Club. She worked there for a time as a hostess where her job was to speak to the men and find out what kind of prostitute they were looking for. She earned £50 per introduction as well as gifts when the punters got to know her. She also

Embassy Club, 7 Old Bond Street, W1S 4PN

used the opportunities to pass on her stolen goods and she said that one of the hostesses regularly gave her 'sugar-daddy,' an eminent QC, clothes stolen in Jermyn Street.

Today this is the Dolce and Gabanna store.

Euston Train Station, Euston Road, NW1 2RT

In January 1954 Shirley was being transferred from Aylesbury prison to Holloway by train. When they arrived at Euston the police car wasn't there to pick them up so they had to wait near the taxi rank. As she was three months pregnant she asked to go to the toilet, and even though there was a police officer outside Shirley escaped through a small window landing back on the platform. She was able to jump in a cab and escape before the police could catch up with her.

St Thomas' Hospital, Westminster Bridge Road, SE1 7EH

Following her escape from Aylesbury prison she was heavily pregnant and had her first child, Joanne, at St Thomas' Hospital. However, as she was on the run she had to be careful about visiting her whilst in the incubator in case she was recognised. She therefore visited whilst wearing a number of disguises. She was caught eight months later at her mother's house.

Astor Club, 57 Berkeley Square, W1J 6ER

In the 1970s Shirley Pitts opened an escort agency on Berkeley Square opposite the famous Astor Club. She had two books running, one for legitimate escorts and one for prostitution. She had both male and female prostitutes and escorts on the books as well as gay and lesbian at a time when homosexuality was criminalised.

In 1975, Charlie Kray was released from prison and was planning to have a benefit party at the Astor. The police filled the other floors of Shirley's building so they could watch who was entering the party. She was worried she was about to be raided when she first saw them arrive. She told the owner of the Astor and all the guests either arrived in disguise or used the back entrance in order to avoid the police.

Tooting Cemetery, Blackstow Road, SW17 0BY

When Shirley Pitts died on March 16, 1992, her funeral was a lavish affair. As the Queen of the Shoplifters there was a parade of 21 Daimlers lining the route to the cemetery. She was buried in a £5k Zandra Rhodes dress which may or may not have been paid for, the Krays sent a wreath with the message 'One of the best', and another message said 'Gone Shopping' in flowers.

Eastcastle Street Robbery (1952)

Eastcastle Street, W1T 3QP

On May 21, 1952, a gang of masked men held up a Royal Mail van carrying High Value Packets (HVP) and escaped with £236,748 10s (£7.3m today). This was the biggest post-war robbery at the time and was led by Billy Hill's gang.

The van had been diverted onto Eastcastle Street due to roadworks on Oxford Street, and the robbers were able to block the van between two vehicles. The robbers pulled the driver, guard and sorter out of the van and beat them before stealing the vehicle.

The van's alarm had been tampered with and the driver hadn't followed protocol with keys. The driver wasn't seriously hurt and it is thought he may have been an insider involved in the robbery.

Augustus Street, NW1 3TJ

The stolen van was then abandoned on Augustus Street with 18 of the 31 mailbags missing.

Despite various leads the crime remains unsolved.

Zoe Progl (1960)

Holloway Prison, Parkhurst Road, N7 0NU

Zoe Progl was a professional burglar and shoplifter, robbing homes and post offices in London, Surrey, Oxfordshire and Brighton and had served several sentences in prison.

Eastcastle Street, W1T 3QP

In 1960 she was sent to Holloway prison after being arrested in Brighton for a robbery. She was sentenced to two and a half years for housebreaking and larceny. However, she had already planned her escape before she was sentenced as this wasn't her first stay there.

On July 24, she put her plan into action. As a model prisoner she

was given a job cleaning offices which gave her access to an outside phoneline where she called her boyfriend Barry Harris to start the plan rolling.

She climbed over a pile of coke to scale the 2.1-metre-high wall. Barry Harris had stashed a metal ladder near the perimeter wall to the east of the prison which allowed him to throw a rope ladder down to Zoe.

She was the first woman to escape from Holloway, but despite dying her hair red she was captured 40 days later and was sentenced to a further 18-months for the escape.

Warwick Square, Pimlico, SW1V 2AA

Zoe Progl lived in a 20-roomed house in Warwick Square which the police called 'The Thieves Retreat' where stolen goods were brought and fenced. The house was regularly raided and on one occasion a stolen 500-weight safe was found in Zoe's room. She was sentenced to 15 months in prison.

We were unable to identify the house number.

Bow Street Magistrates' Court, 4 Bow Street, WC2E 7AT

On August 10, 1960, the police received a call to say she had been spotted in a Chelsea bar. However when they got there she had gone and left a letter to the home secretary saying she would give herself up if the sentence was reduced. On September 7, she was arrested in Notting Hill Gate in bed with Barry.

She appeared at Bow Street following her arrest. She was in Court 3, along with Barry Harris and two friends, Briana O'Malley and Adelaide DeBoer, who were charged with harbouring a fugitive.

Barry, Briana and Adelaide were all given nine months as they had previous convictions. Zoe was given another 18 months.

Bow Street Police Station, 4 Bow Street, WC2E 7AT

Burlington Arcade Smash and Grab (1964)

41 Burlington Arcade, 51 Piccadilly, W1J 0QJ

On June 27, 1964, six masked men drove their Jaguar Mark 10 down the pedestrianised arcade and smashed into the Goldsmiths and Silversmiths Association jewellery shop window. They then stole £35,000 worth of jewellery and reversed the car back out again. People in the offices above threw missiles of flowerpots at the robbers but to no avail.

They have never been caught but it was due to this robbery that the two large bollards now block the entrance to anything other than pedestrians.

Today the store is a Bollingers.

Baker Street Robbery (1971)

Lloyd's Bank, 185 Baker Street, NW1 6XB

On September 1, 1971 three robbers Anthony Gavin, Thomas Stevens and Reginald Tucker, tunnelled into the vaults through the floor of the bank and stole the contents of 260 safety deposit boxes estimated to be worth £3 million (£45m in today's currency). There was a lookout on a rooftop nearby, and they all communicated via walkie talkie.

This was the biggest bank robbery to date and was only to be overshadowed by the Hatton Garden robbery. Nothing has been recovered from the robbery, and many of the security box holders sued Lloyd's Bank for the loss of the contents.

An amateur CB radio operator, Robert Rowlands, picked up the conversations on the walkie talkies used by the robbers from his flat in Wimpole Street. He knew the CB radio only picked up walkie talkies within a couple of miles of his address and contacted the police. At first they didn't believe that he was hearing a bank robbery in progress. When they did finally take notice, they ignored the two-mile radius and tried to target all London banks.

41 Burlington Arcade, 51 Piccadilly, W1J 0QJ

44 | THE TRUE CRIME LOVER'S GUIDE TO LONDON

Lloyd's Bank, 185 Baker Street, NW1 6XB

Le Sac, 189 Baker Street, NW1 6UY
This store was located two doors down from the bank and was leased by the robbers. From there they gathered their equipment and started digging the tunnel under the leather goods store, under the chicken shop next door and into the basement of the bank.

The store was leased by Desmond Wolfe, in his real name, a man already known to the police. He was quickly arrested and the police started looking into his criminal associates, leading to Gavin, Stephens and Tucker's arrests.

Le Sac, 189 Baker Street, NW1 6UY

Old Bailey, EC4M 7EH

In January 1973, all four of the robbers were convicted at the Old Bailey. Wolfe was given eight years, and Gavin, Stephens and Tucker were given 12 years each.

The Security Express Robbery (1983)

At Easter 1983, a gang of robbers waited for the solitary security guard to unlock the gate at the Security Express office on Curtain Road, to get the milk for his morning cuppa, attacked him and bundled him back into the building. The gang who included brothers Jimmy, John and Robbie Knight, John Horsely and Billy Hickson forced him to show how the security controls worked and as the staff started arriving they were each taken hostage by the gang.

The gang were able to get away with £6m in cash.

The original building is no longer there.

The Fox, 28 Paul Street, Shoreditch, EC2A 4LB

www.thefoxpublichouse.co.uk

John Horsley hid the sacks of money in his garage and also built a false back into a cupboard at his father-in-law's flat where he hid a further £270,000 for Hicks. A false wall was discovered by police at John Knight's pub, The Fox, where some of the cash had been stored. The pub had once been managed by Clifford Saxe who was also involved in the robbery.

The hole smelt of mildew and old beer which matched the smell on some of the recovered money.

When John was arrested his brother Ronnie, who was once married to Barbara Windsor, fled to Spain.

Luton Airport, Airport Way, Luton LU2 9LY

When Ronnie Knight returned to the UK ten years later, he was arrested on the tarmac at Luton airport for his part in the robbery.

Old Bailey, EC4M 7EH

At trial, Horsley was sentenced to eight years and was described as the gang's banker. John Knight was given 22 years for his part in arranging the robbery. Other gang members James Knight, Freddie Foreman and Clifford Saxe each received eight years.

On January 4, 1995 Ronnie Knight was sentenced to seven years for handling £314,813 of stolen money.

Brink's-Mat Robbery (1983)

On November 26, 1983, a robbery took place at one of Britain's most secure vaults in Heathrow. This amounted to the biggest heist in UK history worth £520m (in modern money) of gold bullion. It is thought that any gold jewellery from the 1990s probably included some of the Brink's-Mat gold.

To this day, only a third of the bullion has been recovered and criminal gangs are still trying to locate it.

Heathrow International Trading Estate, Unit 7, Green Lane, Hounslow, TW4 6HB

At the Heathrow Trading Estate, the robbers Micky McAvoy, Brian Robinson, Tony White, Brian Perry and George Francis pointed semi-automatic pistols in the faces of the security guards until the two with the combination opened the safe.

Inside there were 6,800 gold bars, weighing 3.5 tonnes, as well as money, travellers cheques and diamonds. The bars hadn't all been loaded into the safe as there wasn't room and it is thought the robbers weren't expecting so much. Witness statements comment about the low suspension on their getaway van as it struggled with 3.5 tonnes of gold.

West Drayton Police Station, Station Road, Uxbridge, UB7 7JQ

Brian Robinson was taken to West Drayton Police Station where he provided what appeared to be a solid alibi.

Chiswick Police Station, 209-211 Chiswick High Road, W4 2DU

Micky McAvoy was interviewed at Chiswick Police Station where he also refused to give any answers.

Cowcross Street, EC1M 6BY

Noye and Reader met a number of associates in a café on Cowcross Street opposite the station and exchanged a number of packages which were then put into Reader's car.

Royal National Hotel, 38-51 Bedford Way, WC1H 0DG

On January 9, 1985 Flying Squad followed Reader to this hotel where he met Christopher Weyman and Tommy Adams in the lobby. Ten minutes later they drove off. Reader met with the jewellers a number of times here returning to Noye's Kent home afterwards.

Paddington Station, Praed Street, W2 1HU

The police followed Adams and Weyman to Paddington Station where they bought first class tickets to Swindon. Adams was carrying a very heavy brown suitcase and they both appeared to be agitated. They returned to Paddington later that evening with Adams carrying a different suitcase.

Old Bailey, EC4M 7EH

On October 25, 1984 White, McAvoy and Robinson were charged at the Old Bailey with conspiring to commit robbery and the actual robbery. They all pleaded not guilty. On December 1, the jury came back with the verdict of not guilty for Tony White, and guilty for Brian Robinson and Micky McAvoy. They were both sentenced to 25 years in prison.

Royal National Hotel, 38-51 Bedford Way, WC1H 0DG

The Old Bailey was also the location in May 1986 for Kenny Noye's and six others' trial for handling the Brink's-Mat gold and conspiracy to evade VAT where he was found guilty and sentenced to fourteen years.

Millennium Dome Raid (2000)

Millennium Dome, SE10 0BB

On November 7, 2000, an exhibition at the Dome was displaying the Millennium Star diamond, which was worth £200 million.

A gang, armed with smoke bombs, ammonia, a nail gun and a sledgehammer drove a JCB into the Dome in order to break into the vault. They planned to make a getaway by boat down the Thames.

However, the police had been tipped off and surrounded the Dome the night before. There were more than 200 officers, including 60 armed flying squad, and 20 on the river. The diamond had also been replaced with a fake.

Old Bailey, EC4M 7EH

Five of the robbers Lee Wenham, Raymond Betson, Aldo Ciarrocchi, Robert Adams, Kevin Meredith and William Cockram, were caught and received between four and eighteen years at their trial which started on November 8, 2001.

Graff Diamonds Robbery (2009)

Graff Diamonds, 6-7 New Bond Street, W1S 3SJ

On August 6, 2009 at 4:40pm two men, Craig Calderwood and Aman Kassaye, entered the Graff diamonds store posing as customers. They pulled out two handguns and stole 43 items of jewellery worth £40m.

They had used a professional make-up artist to disguise their features with latex meaning they were unrecognisable so they hadn't hidden their faces from the cameras. They held one of the assistants, Petra Ehnar, hostage in order to leave the store, releasing her in the street outside as they escaped in a blue BMW.

The two men were arrested during the getaway, as one of the robbers left their mobile phone behind which enabled police to identify them.

None of the stolen items have been found, even though all the diamonds were laser-inscribed with the Graff logo.

Westminster Magistrates' Court, 181 Marylebone Road, NW1 5BR

On August 22, Clinton Mogg, Calderwood and another man Solomun Beyene were all held at Westminster Magistrates' Court before appearing at Kingston Crown Court.

Woolwich Crown Court, 2 Belmarsh Way, SE28 0EY

On August 7, 2010 Aman Kasseye, was found guilty of conspiracy to rob, possession of a firearm and kidnap and was sentenced to 23 years in prison.

Beyene, Mogg and Thomas were each given 16 years for conspiracy to rob. Calderwood was given 21 years.

Hatton Garden Heist (2015)

Paris Jewels (was Hatton Garden Safety Deposit Ltd), 88-90 Hatton Garden, EC1N 8PN

Overnight on April 2, 2015, a gang of elderly gangsters decided on one last job and attempted to rob Hatton Garden Safety Deposit Ltd.

The gang were Danny Jones, 58, Terry Perkins, 67, Brian Reader, 76, who was imprisoned as part of the Brink's-Mat Robbery, John 'Kenny' Collins, 75, Michael Seed, 62, Carl Wood, 58, Hugh Doyle, 48, William 'Billy the Fish' Lincoln, 60, and Jon Harbinson, 42.

Late on April 2, they drilled a large hole through the vault wall, before their pump broke, giving them the option of giving up or finding a solution. They made the decision to buy a new pump and then returned the next night to finish the job which they did, getting away with between £14m and £24m worth of jewels, gold and cash.

Paris Jewels (was Hatton Garden Safety Deposit Ltd), 88-90 Hatton Garden, EC1N 8PN

Madison, 25 Hatton Garden, EC1N 8BQ

Kenny used the first-floor corner office of 25 Hatton Garden, as a lookout point throughout the robbery, as it gave clear views of the front and the side of the building on Greville Street. However, after getting fish and chips, Kenny fell asleep and failed to warn the gang that the security guard had been alerted by the alarm. Luckily for the gang, the guard thought it was a false alarm and went home.

The next night when the gang returned to finish the job, Kenny did exactly the same thing and was woken by Basil who went to see why he wasn't answering the radio.

Castle Pub, 54 Pentonville Road, N1 9HF

www.thecastleislington.co.uk

Danny, Terry and Kenny met here regularly from as early as 2012 to plan the heist.

Madison, 25 Hatton Garden, EC1N 8BQ

Scotti's Snack Bar, 38 Clerkenwell Green, EC1R 0DU

Terry and Danny met here every Friday to reminisce about old times and catch up.

14 Bletsoe Walk, Islington, N1 7HZ

Kenny lived here, and was dropped off on April 3, once the pump had broken meaning they were unable to carry on with the robbery. Once the robbery had been completed on the morning of April 4, the stolen jewellery was stored overnight here in the wheelie bins it had been placed in within the vault.

Ye Olde Cherry Tree Pub, The Green, N14 6EN

www.vintageinn.co.uk/restaurants/london/yeoldecherrytreesouthgate

On April 24, Danny, Terry and Kenny met up here to discuss selling the loot and how to make the handovers.

The Castle Farringdon Pub, 34-35 Cowcross Street, EC1M 6DB

www.thecastlefarringdon.co.uk

On May 1, Kenny and Terry met Brian Reader here. It was the first meeting with Brian since the robbery and it was tense. It was here, that the police recorded the meeting and employed a lip reader to interpret what they were saying.

Delhi Grill, 21 Chapel Market, N1 9EZ

This was another favourite meeting place of Terry, Kenny and Danny as they believed the hustle and bustle of the busy restaurant meant sensitive conversations would go unheard.

Belmarsh Prison, Western Way, SE28 0EB

The gang were sent here while they were awaiting trial.

Woolwich Crown Court, 2 Belmarsh Way, SE28 0EY

The trial of John (Kenny) Collins, Daniel Jones, Brian Reader, Michael Seed and Terry Perkins was held here. They all pleaded guilty to the charge of conspiracy to commit burglary and all were sentenced to seven years in prison with Seed getting ten years.

Carl Wood, William (Billy) Hill, Jon Harbinson and Hugh Doyle, were all charged with conspiracy to commit burglary and conspiracy to conceal, convert or transfer criminal property.

A confiscation order was added to all their sentences if they were unable to pay back what was stolen: Seed, Jones and Collins got an extra six and a half years. Terry died in prison in 2018, and Reader was released but could be recalled as part of the confiscation order.

Harbinson was acquitted, Carl Wood was given six years prison sentence, and Hugh Doyle was given a suspended sentence.

Edmonton Cemetery, Church Street, N9 9HP

Danny Jones told the police when he was in prison that he had buried his share of the loot in the cemetery. He said he had buried it in two graves of male relatives of his wife, Val Hart, but would only reveal both of them when he was released.

The police were able to recover some of the stolen jewellery from the memorial stone of his father-in-law, Sidney James Hart. They didn't tell Danny of their discovery, and when they took him to the cemetery on October 15, 2015 he led them to the grave of Sidney John Hart, where a smaller stash was uncovered. He was adamant this was all the jewellery there was.

Goldman Sachs Theft (2004)

Peterborough Court, Fleet Street, EC4A 2BB

In 2004, personal assistant Joyti De-Laurey stole £4.3m from her bosses' bank accounts at Goldman Sachs. She worked for Jennifer Moses and her husband Ron Beller, and then later Scott Mead.

Woolwich, 88 Fleet Street, EC4Y 1DH

As part of Joyti's role she was often expected to forge her boss' signature, and she wondered if they would notice money going missing. In 2000, she wrote a cheque for £4,000 and cashed it in the Woolwich on Fleet Street. Jennifer Moses didn't notice the cash was missing.

Joyti kept cashing cheques until in 2001 she transferred £2.1m in one go. None of her bosses noticed the money was gone.

In total, she stole £3.3m from Scott Mead and £1.1m from Jennifer Moses.

Southwark Crown Court, 1 English Grounds, SE1 2HU

Eventually, she was arrested in 2004 for fraud and was tried at Southwark Crown Court.

She claimed the money she took from Scott Mead was 'hush money' for helping to cover up affairs which he denied. In January 2004 she was sentenced to seven years in prison, even though the average for this crime was three and a half years. She was released in 2007.

Her husband and mother were also charged and sentenced for money laundering; her husband received a six-month sentence and her mother a suspended sentence.

6

BODY SNATCHERS

During the early nineteenth century a new crime of body snatching arose due to an increase in the number of schools of surgery and anatomy where students required human bodies to learn their craft. The bodies of executed criminals were often handed over to them by the state, but demand outstripped the supply.

Therefore a class of resurrection men developed, who stalked cemeteries at night and dug up recent graves, removed the bodies and then sold them to the anatomy schools. The theft of the body itself was not a crime, as no one could own a body, so they were careful not to steal anything from the grave such as shrouds or the coffin itself. Although not strictly illegal, resurrection men were not well-respected members of society as what they did was considered desecration of a body.

Tyburn (Marble Arch), W1C 1LX
Resurrectionists were known to grab the bodies from the gallows at Tyburn, whilst they were still warm in order to sell them to the anatomy schools. Although the bodies of criminals who were executed were often handed over to the anatomists anyway, the resurrectionists' behaviour was known to have sparked riots with the onlookers who were there to watch the execution.

Tyburn (Marble Arch), W1C 1LX

St George the Martyr, Borough High Street, SE1 1JA

www.stgeorge-themartyr.co.uk

In 1777, a body snatcher attempted to steal a corpse from the graveyard at St George the Martyr and was caught. This was the first prosecution for body snatching to take place, although it was a crime which was well-known at the time.

Alderney Road Cemetery, Stepney, E1 4EG

This cemetery was very aware it could be the victim of the resurrection men before its closure in 1852.

When burials were carried out here, a wheeled sentry-box was used and moved around the cemetery so family members could keep an eye on new burials for a number of nights after the burial had taken place.

Globe Fields, Whitechapel (Now Globe Road Memorial Gardens), E2 0LE

In October 1839 police were called to this burial ground after a witness working for the Eastern Counties Railway Company, saw two men and a boy digging up bodies in one part of the burial ground and throwing them into a large pit they had dug on the other side.

The police found the hole filled to within eight inches from the top, and the coffins had all been stripped of metal. It was common to chop up coffins to sell the wood and nails, but also to make room for more burials in the churchyards which provided an income for the church.

One of the bodies had only been in the ground for about six weeks. These were not resurrection men, but thieves.

The police pulled over a young lad with a bag of nails and human bones which he claimed he was going to sell.

Globe Fields is currently a memorial garden next to the Victory Life Baptist Church.

Crossbones Cemetery, Union Street, SE1 1SD

www.crossbones.org.uk

Between the sixteenth century and 1853, this unconsecrated burial ground was used "for the interment of the low women who frequented the neighbourhood" and then for the paupers and those who were forbidden to be buried in a churchyard.

There were so many burials here that in the 1850s the bodies were buried close enough to the surface that hands and feet were often seen poking through the sod.

It was a favourite place for body-snatchers to come and remove the bodies shortly after burial to sell to the anatomy schools.

It was closed as a burial ground in 1853 due to the overcrowding and the land sold in 1883 for development but has since been set up as a memorial site.

7

MURDER

London has unfortunately been the location of thousands of murders over the years. Between 1921 and 1958 there were 1,674 murders with only 19 being the victims of serial killers.

Sadly, we often know more about the murderers than the victims. The victims were generally ordinary people, unremarkable, possibly poor or in prostitution and therefore hadn't made much impact on the world at large.

However following arrest, the murderers are interviewed, examined by psychiatrists, put on trial and reported on regularly in the newspapers. They themselves may not have been remarkable either, but their actions were unusual and therefore considered interesting and newsworthy.

4th Baron Mohun (1692)

Leicester Square, WC2H 7LU
On December 9, 1692 the 4th Baron Mohun, Charles Mohun, along with Richard Hill ambushed an actor William Mountfort in Leicester Square and stabbed him, killing him.

Leicester Square at the time was known as Leicester Fields and was a residential area, which had been constructed in 1670.

Leicester Square, WC2H 7LU

MURDER | 57

The modern square in the middle is likely to be on the original footprint.

House of Lords, Houses of Parliament, Parliament Square, SW1A 0PW
Richard Hill fled following the murder, and Mohun was arrested and tried at the House of Lords, due to his status. He was acquitted on February 6, 1693.

Hyde Park, W1J 7NT
Mohun himself was killed in a duel on November 15, 1712 in Hyde Park. He challenged the Duke of Hamilton to a

duel following a dispute regarding an inheritance. The Duke of Hamilton 'won' resulting in Mohun's death but he was then murdered by Mohun's second, General George MacCartney.

Catherine Hayes (1726)

St Margaret's Church, St Margaret Street, SW1P 3JX

On March 5, 1726, a head was found in the Thames at Horseferry. The constables of the watch were unable to identify it so they popped it on a spike in the churchyard hoping that someone would step forward with information.

There were two false leads where it was identified as the head of a local criminal gang member, and the husband of a woman (although he was found to be alive and living in Deptford).

Then a body was found on March 26 in a pond near Tyburn Road, which was identified as John Hayes.

Old Bailey, EC4M 7EH

His wife Catherine Hayes and her lovers Thomas Wood and Thomas Billings were arrested for his murder and were held in Newgate which was destroyed in 1904 and replaced with the modern Old Bailey. They both said that Catherine had asked them to do it. They got John drunk and when he collapsed they hit him with an axe.

The story developed further when it was uncovered that Thomas Billings was Catherine's illegitimate

son conceived when she worked for John Hayes' father, meaning he had actually killed his step-father and brother.

Hayes, Wood and Billings were sentenced to death at the Old Bailey which was the courthouse next to Newgate on April 30. Hayes was sentenced to being burned alive without being strangled beforehand as was the norm.

Tyburn, W1H 7EL

Wood died of gaol fever before the sentence could be carried out but on May 14, 1726 Hayes and Billings joined a procession of highwaymen, sodomites and burglars to Tyburn from Newgate.

Watching a woman burn to death was a big draw for spectators and paid seats were an easy way to make quick money. Unfortunately a quickly erected set of pews collapsed killing twelve people.

The Temple Murder (1733)

Temple, EC4Y 9DA

On February 15, 1733 Sarah Malcolm murdered three people at the Temple.

She was a charwoman at the Inns of Court and strangled her employer, Lydia Duncome, her companion, Mrs Harrison and a maidservant Ann, by slitting her throat. When a neighbour, Mrs Love arrived for an appointment and received no answer she persuaded a laundress to climb through the fourth-floor window, where she discovered the bodies.

Sarah also stole £300 of jewellery, cash and plate.

Old Bailey, EC4M 7EH
Sarah was arrested after stolen items and blood-stained clothes were found in her lodgings. She was arrested along with her lover Mary Tracey and Mary's brothers James and William Alexander.

On February 23, 1733 Sarah was tried for the murders and was found guilty within fifteen minutes and sentenced to death. The Alexander brothers and Mary Tracey were released without charge.

Mitre Court/Fetter Lane, EC4Y 1BN
Sarah Malcolm was hanged for the murders here. People were so intrigued by her that they paid to see her body at the undertakers and one man paid half-a-crown to kiss her corpse.

Ratcliff Highway Murders (1811)

In December 1811, two families were murdered on the Ratcliffe Highway some 12 days apart. The murders were carried out with a sailor's knife, a mallet, chisel, crowbar, and shipwright's hammer. The first family was found on 29 Ratcliff Highway (now The Highway) which has since been rebuilt. Linen draper Timothy Marr, his wife Celia, apprentice James Gowan and baby son were found at the back of this building. The baby was 14 weeks old, and his throat had been cut as he slept in the cradle. The servant Margaret Jewell was out on errands to get oysters for their tea when the attacks happened.

The second family comprised John Williamson, a 56-year-old publican, Elizabeth, his 60-year-old wife; and their servant, Bridget Anna Harrington. They were found in the King's Arms pub, on New Gravel Lane. All three had serious head injuries and their throats had been slashed. The pub was demolished in the 1830s.

St George-in-the-East Church, 14 Cannon St Road, E1 0BH
The memorial for the seven victims was held in the parish church of St George-in-the-East. The baby had been baptised here only three months earlier.

Corner of Cable Street and Cannon Street Road, E1 0BL
The Irish or Scottish sailor, John Williams, was charged with the murder but the evidence was flimsy. He was very likely innocent.

He hanged himself in police custody before he was put on trial.

As he killed himself he was unable to be buried in consecrated ground as suicide was illegal at this time. It was traditional to bury suicides at a crossroads as a means to baffle the ghost who wouldn't know which way to turn.

Above: *St George-in-the-East Church, 14 Cannon Street Road, E1 0BH*

Left: *Crown and Dolphin Pub, 56 Cannon Street Road, E1 0BL*

John Williams was therefore, buried in a shallow grave on the corner of Cable Street and Cannon Street Road with a stake through his heart. The body remained there until 1886 when workmen installing new gas mains uncovered it.

Crown and Dolphin Pub, 56 Cannon Street Road, E1 0BL

It was rumoured that the landlord of the Crown and Dolphin pub kept the head of John Williams behind the bar.

This pub was closed in 2002 and has been converted into residential use.

John Mortland (1823)

Montagu Square, W1H 2LB

On April 7, 1823, John (aka Joseph) Mortland murdered poet Sir Warwick Bampfylde in Montagu Square. He then killed himself.

Mortland had been a servant working for Bampfylde and was jealous as his wife still worked there and he believed the 70-year-old Bampfylde was having an affair with her.

The bullet got stuck in Bampfylde's ribs, and he died two weeks later of gangrene as some fabric from his braces had entered the wound.

Mortland was buried at a crossroads which is now a small triangle of unconsecrated ground opposite Lord's Cricket Ground with a stake through his heart. Suicide was considered illegal and it was thought their ghosts would return hence they were staked to the grave and buried at a crossroads. His was the last crossroads burial.

The Italian Boy (1831)

Carlo Ferrier was 14 years old and earned money by charging people to watch his performing white mice. On November 4, 1831 John Bishop and Thomas Williams lured him away from Smithfield with promise of work.

They murdered Carlo by feeding him rum laced with laudanum and hanging him upside down in a well until he drowned.

They then sold his teeth to a dentist and his body was hawked around the London hospitals looking for the best price. A man called James May became involved at this point.

Before execution John Bishop confessed that the boy wasn't Carlo Ferrier but a Lincolnshire cattle driver.

Quadrant Arcade, Regent Street, W1B 5RL

One witness, Mary Paragelli, at the trial at the Old Bailey stated she had last seen little Carlo Ferrier at the Quadrant in Regent Street a few days before his death.

Guy's Hospital, SE1 9GU

The murderers had taken Carlo's body to Guy's Hospital hoping to sell it but it was refused.

72 Dean Street, W1D 3SG

They also went to Joseph Carpue's anatomy school on Dean Street. After determining how fresh the body was Carpue offered eight guineas and Bishop agreed to bring the body the next day. However, after a chat in the pub with resurrection men, Bishop was told he could get more money, so never delivered the body to Carpue.

King's College School of Anatomy, Strand, WC2R 2LS

On November 5, 1831, the fresh corpse of Carlo was brought here by Bishop and May, who wanted twelve guineas for it. They were given nine.

When the demonstrator of anatomy studied the body he realised it had not been buried and called the police.

Bishop, Williams and May were arrested, and on November 8, a coroners' jury was held, declaring "wilful murder against some person or persons unknown".

St Paul's Church (Watch House), Bedford Street, WC2E 9ED

The body of the boy was taken to St Paul's Watch House on November 6, 1831 to be examined and to determine the cause of death.

The watch house stood to the left of the entrance gateway, approached by the steps and filled the gap between the gateway and NatWest.

Bow Street Magistrates' Court, 4 Bow Street, WC2E 7AT

During the magistrates' court proceedings at Bow Street, a crowd of hundreds of people had gathered outside. As Bishop and May (who was later pardoned) left the court they were jostled and jeered by the crowd as they were taken to Newgate resulting in injury to Bishop's shoulder.

Old Bailey, EC4M 7EH

The three prisoners appeared at the Old Bailey between December 2 and 3, 1831. They were all found guilty and sentenced to death.

Bishop and Williams were hanged on December 5 outside Newgate but May was later acquitted. Bishop admitted to selling between 500 and 1,000 bodies since 1819.

Attempted Murder (1825)

Sheen's Burial Ground, 52-58 Commercial Road and 109-153 Back Church Lane, E1 1LP

On July 23, 1825, a man was thrown into a grave at this private burial ground in an attempt to bury him alive.

The day before, his wife Lucer had died in hospital following what appeared to be a severe beating. The inquest found she had died of natural

Sheen's Burial Ground, 52-58 Commercial Road and 109-153 Back Church Lane, E1 1LP

causes, but neighbours and friends knew her husband was guilty of murder.

He refused to have her buried according to Irish and Catholic tradition which saw her funeral at Sheen's Burial Ground. As her body was lowered into the grave, the 8-10,000 strong crowd attempted to throw him in as well. The Lambeth-Street police intervened in time and whisked the man away.

The burial ground has been turned into green space in front of large-scale blocks of flats between Gower's Walk and Back Church Lane.

Whitechapel Road Murder (1874)

(Hen & Chickens) 54 Borough High Street, SE1 1XL

The police discovered Henry Wainwright at 54 Borough High Street, clutching a parcel containing the dismembered body of Harriet Louisa Lane, in 1874.

Harriet, aged 23, was a milliner's apprentice when she met Wainwright. She had been Wainwright's mistress since 1871, and they had two daughters together. She called herself Mrs Percy King.

Wainwright was taking the body into his brother, Thomas Wainwright's ironmongery shop at the Hen and Chickens on Borough High Street when he was apprehended.

The building is now an estate agents.

40 Tredegar Square, Bow, E3 5AE

Henry Wainwright lived with his wife and four children at number 40.

(Hen & Chickens) 54 Borough High Street, SE1 1XL

84 Whitechapel Road, E1 1DT

Henry Wainwright, 36, a brush manufacturer, had a warehouse at this address. This was near the Pavilion Theatre, which Wainwright frequented.

215 Whitechapel Road, E1 1DE

Opposite the shop was the warehouse for Wainwright's brush-making business.

Wainwright killed Harriet at his shop, burying her beneath the floor of the paint room, covered in quicklime. Local workmen had heard gunshots between 5pm and 6pm, but thought it was a local eccentric who was known to have fired a gun at times. A post-mortem on the

215 Whitechapel Road, E1 1DE

scared to confront him so he followed the cab and called a policeman.

Today Henry's shop is Mahir (London) clothes shop.

3 Sidney Square, Mile End Road, E1 2EY

Wainwright moved Harriet and the children to a house on Sidney Square, as he was in spiralling debt and found financing two households difficult. Harriet had been asking him more frequently for money, often at his shop, as her allowance was being reduced. She was forced to take lodgings here at the house belonging to Mrs Foster.

On the night of September 11, 1874 she arranged for someone to look after the children, and left Sidney Square

remains showed she had been shot in the head and then had her throat cut.

A year later, on September 11, 1875 with his brother, Thomas Wainwright, they removed the body and dismembered it to make disposal easier.

When Henry was moving the body from his shop he asked a friend, Alfred Phillip Stokes, to help him. He also told him he had a hammer, shovel and chopper which he would give Stokes to sell on.

Stokes became suspicious of two badly smelling parcels and when Wainwright went to get a cab, he looked inside one and saw a human head. Wainwright returned with the cab, and Stokes was too

3 Sidney Square, Mile End Road, E1 2EY

with her night clothes in a bundle. When her friends became worried about her, Wainwright said she had travelled to Brighton and was going to live abroad with a man, Edward Frieake. This man was actually an auctioneer friend of Wainwright and knew nothing about Harriet. Wainwright claimed it was a coincidence that they had the same name.

Old Bailey, EC4M 7EH
Henry and Thomas Wainwright (so-called Frieake) were tried at the Old Bailey in November 1875. Henry claimed a 'man in the pub' had paid him to dispose of the parcels and he didn't know what was in them.

W.S. Gilbert (from Gilbert and Sullivan), in order to avoid jury duty acted as a junior barrister for the defence at his trial.

Thomas was given seven years imprisonment as an accessory after the fact, and Henry was hanged outside Newgate on December 21, 1875.

Castle Street Murder (1878)

Old Castle Street (was Castle Alley), Whitechapel, E6 1PP

On Saturday June 1, 1878, the body of 19-month-old Elizabeth Lazerus was discovered close to the washhouse on Castle Alley, on a doorstep close to her parents' home. Her father, Simon, a tailor, who lived at 4 Old Castle Street, said she had gone missing on the

Old Castle Street (was Castle Alley), Whitechapel, E6 1PP

Wednesday at 6pm after she had been let into the street to play.

Her body was brought to her home on Saturday at 1:30am, with the top half of her body soaked through. She had drowned, and there was evidence of lime and sand on the body. The washhouse was undergoing building works at the time and it was thought she died on the site.

Peter Wincey, the watchman, was known for chasing children who annoyed him with his stick and he was arrested for the murder but was later bailed. The only evidence against him was someone who looked like him was seen near the area, and some odd, distressed things he had said to the parents. The case was dismissed and to this day there is doubt as to whether she was murdered or died in an accident.

The washhouse building is particularly interesting as it is now just the façade of the original washhouse with a completely new building behind.

Turner Street Murder (1896)

31 Turner Street, E1 2AS

John Goodman Levy, a Jewish fence, was murdered at this address on April 4, 1896. During the morning, the housekeeper Annie Gale was seen opening the shutters and talking to the dairyman.

At 1pm, Miss Laughton arrived for lunch following an invitation from Mr Levy but received no answer when she knocked. She called on a neighbour, William Schafer to see what was happening. He went around the back and

31 Turner Street, E1 2AS

saw a man bent over in the outhouse, who fled into the basement when he realised he had been seen.

Mr Levy was found murdered in the outhouse, and the housekeeper Mrs Gale was found dead in the top floor front bedroom. They had both been hit with a hammer, before having their throats cut.

When the police arrived, there was a disturbance when it was realised the murderer, William Seaman, had made his way through a hole in the ceiling into the attic and was on the roof. He stepped onto the parapet and fell 40 feet to the ground. A small girl broke his fall.

The top floor of the building as it currently stands is a modern addition.

London Hospital, Whitechapel Road, E1 1FR

Seaman was taken to the hospital with a fractured arm, along with the little girl. It was only when he was at the hospital that he was identified.

He had not long been out of prison and had told a prisoner before his release 'There's a bloody fence and his whore at Whitechapel that owe me £70 pounds on a deal. I'm going to their place for the money when I get out and if the old bugger squeals at paying I'll put his light out sure enough.' There was no evidence that Mr Levy owed Seaman any money.

Thames Police Court, 79 Aylward Street, Stepney Green, E1 0QH

Seaman was charged here for larceny and two counts of murder. He was

London Hospital, Whitechapel Road, E1 1FR

carried into the courtroom seated in an armchair wincing in pain.

Seaman was executed along with two other unrelated criminals on June 9, 1896 at Newgate Prison.

Emily Dimmock (1907)

29 Agar Grove (was St Paul's Road), NW1 9UG

Emily Dimmock (aka Phyllis) was murdered on September 11, 1907. She was working as a prostitute, although her husband, Bertram Shaw, wasn't aware of her profession. She worked when he was on night shifts.

Emily Dimmock and her husband lived at this address, and this was where her body was found.

The Rocket (was Rising Sun), 120 Euston Road, NW1 2AL
www.therocketeustonroad.co.uk

Emily met some of her clients in this pub, including Robert Wood, an artist who worked for the London Sand Blast Decorative Glass Works on Gray's Inn Road. He was eventually charged with her murder, however, he was acquitted and the murder was never solved.

Old Eagle Pub, 251 Royal College Street, NW1 9LU

On the night of her murder, September 11, 1907 Emily had spent time in this pub before heading to her home on Agar Grove. The killer entered

MURDER | 71

her home and slit her throat whilst she slept.

Dr Crippen (1910)

Dr Crippen was married to Cora (aka Belle Elmore). He was American and his Drs qualifications were not recognised in the UK so he worked for Munnions, a patented medical company. Cora wanted to be a singer but wasn't very talented.

He was having an affair with Ethel Le Neve. On January 31, 1910 after a party Crippen killed his wife at Hilldrop Crescent (the building has long been demolished), either through poison (hyoscine) or some reports say a shot was heard.

He initially told people Cora had returned to the US for a family death, which then changed to she had died there. When a police officer questioned him, saying that the death wasn't registered in the US he changed his story again and said she wasn't dead but had left him.

In the meantime, Ethel had moved in and started wearing Cora's clothes and jewellery. Crippen then left for Canada with Ethel disguised as a boy.

The dismembered body of Cora was found in the cellar of Hilldrop Crescent covered in quicklime. She was identified by a piece of flesh from her abdomen which had a scar.

Aboard Crippen's ship the SS *Montrose* heading to Canada, a wireless telegraph was used to contact Scotland Yard about two suspicious passengers on board. The English police got a boat which arrived in Canada two days before the *Montrose*.

Crippen and Le Neve were arrested and returned on the sister ship to take them back to Liverpool. They were the first criminals to be caught by wireless telegraph.

2 Bucknall Street, WC2H 8LA

This was the site for Lewis and Burrows Ltd Chemist where in January 1910 Crippen bought five grains of hyoscine hydrobromide. As it was such a large amount it had to be ordered from the wholesalers and collected a few days later. It wasn't questioned due to his medical credentials.

Old Bailey, EC4M 7EH

Both Crippen and Ethel Le Neve were charged at the Old Bailey on October 18, 1910, with the murder of Cora on February 1, 1910. He pleaded not guilty.

However, Crippen was found guilty and sentenced to death. He was executed on November 23, 1910. Ethel le Neve was acquitted.

Pentonville Prison, Caledonian Road, N7 8TT

Crippen was hanged at Pentonville on November 23, 1910 and was buried in the prison grounds.

Eltham Common Murder (1918)

The Fireworks Factory (was Woolwich Arsenal Works), 11 No. 1 Street, Royal Arsenal, SE18 6HD
www.woolwich.works

Nellie Grace Trew, worked here when she was only 16. She was known to all as Peg.
Woolwich Works is a now multi-disciplinary cultural hub which opened in 2021.

Eltham Common (near Eltham Woolwich Road), SE9 6UA
On the morning on Sunday February 10, the body of Nellie Trew was found on the common. She had been raped and strangled. The night before, she had left her home to go to the library and never returned.
A button and a piece of wire were found near the body.

Hewson Manufacturing Company, Newman Passage, W1T 1EG
David Greenwood worked for this company and his co-worker Ted Farrell recognised the button as coming from his coat. He tried to deny it, but the wire found near the site of the body was a spring part used at Hewson's. Greenwood was arrested.

Old Bailey, EC4M 7EH
Greenwood's trial started on April 24, 1918. He pleaded not guilty and said he wasn't wearing the coat at the time.

He was found guilty, but because of his young age he avoided the death penalty and instead spent 15 years in prison and was released in 1933 when he was 36.

Finborough Road Murder (1922)

Wizards and Wonders (was Lyons Corner House), 13 Coventry Street (corner of Rupert Street), W1D 7AG
When in London, Ronald True visited the Lyons Corner House in Leicester Square where he met good friend James Armstrong. Many of the women he met thought he was insane. He bought a pistol from Armstrong in order to 'protect' himself from the 'other Ronald True' who he believed was his alter ego who carried out his crimes.

13a Finborough Road, SW10 9DF
Prostitute Olive Young (real name Gertrude Yates) lived in the basement flat at number 13. Ronald True stayed overnight at her flat and stole £5 from her when he left. She swore she wouldn't see him again but he kept visiting and calling her.
On March 2, 3 and 4 he had driven to her house but she was out. However, she was in on March 5 and he spent the night with her.
On March 6, about 7:30 in the morning, he made them both a cup of tea and as she sat up in bed to drink it he beat her to death. She was only 25.

Wizards and Wonders (was Lyons Corner House), 13 Coventry Street (corner of Rupert Street), W1D 7AG

He told the daily, Emily Steel, when she arrived at 9:15 not to disturb Olive as she was still sleeping. True stayed at the house until about 9:50. Olive's body was discovered at about 10:15.

Grand Hotel, Northumberland Avenue, WC2N 5BY
On March 2, Ronald True stayed at this hotel, and they found him a chauffeur to drive him around. None of it was paid for.

21 & 27 Wardour Street, W1D 6PN
After the murder he took his taxi to Wardour Street where he got a shave at

Right: *Grand Hotel, Northumberland Avenue, WC2N 5BY*

Below left and below right: *21 & 27 Wardour Street, W1D 6PN*

number 21, and then at number 27 he pawned two rings.

Today Number 21 is Café TPT and number 27 is Hungs on the corner of Rupert Court.

Brixton Prison, Jebb Avenue, Brixton Hill, SW2 5XF

When True was arrested he was put under observation in Brixton prison hospital, but he was still able to attack another prisoner.

Old Bailey, EC4M 7EH

His trial started at the Old Bailey on May 1, 1922. He was examined by two psychiatrists who agreed with the prison doctor that he had a congenital mental disorder which was exacerbated by drug use.

Back in 1915, True had joined the Royal Flying Corps but crashed on his first flight suffering a severe concussion. A month later he crashed again and a head injury left him mentally impaired.

The jury however found him guilty, but not insane and he was sentenced to death. However, after appeal he was sent to Broadmoor Criminal Lunatic Asylum (later Broadmoor Institution) where he died in 1951.

Savoy Murder (1923)

Savoy Hotel, Strand, WC2R 0EZ

On July 10, 1923 the night porter heard three gunshots, and saw a young woman, Madame Marguerite Fahmy,

Savoy, Strand, WC2R 0EZ

throw a gun to the floor in front of a man, her Egyptian husband Prince Ali Fahmy Bey who was slumped in the corner. She was heard to say repeatedly in French 'What have I done, my dear?'

Throughout their stay there had been violent public rows and evidence of physical violence by both husband and wife.

Old Bailey, EC4M 7EH

The trial was held at the Old Bailey, and the attraction of royalty ensured a packed public gallery. As her husband was said to have 'perverted practices' and 'never treated Madame normally,' coupled with evidence that Marguerite had visited the doctor at the Savoy with anal injuries, the jury found her not guilty of murder in less than an hour.

The prosecution were not allowed to question Marguerite, otherwise they would have found out she was a high-class prostitute and like her husband favoured same sex relationships.

Charing Cross Trunk Murder (1927)

Sydney Street, Chelsea, SW3 6PX
Minnie Bonati was last seen alive on Sydney Street on May 4, between 3:45 and 4pm.

86 Rochester Row, SW1P 1LJ
John Robinson, an estate agent, worked in a second-floor office at this address. He hailed a taxi from outside the office and got the driver to help him carry a heavy trunk from the office. He then went to Charing Cross Station.

His building was directly opposite the old police station on Rochester Row and has since been rebuilt.

Charing Cross Station, Strand, WC2N 5HF
On May 6, 1927 John Robinson left a large trunk at the left luggage office before jumping into a taxi and leaving. The following Monday staff noticed the trunk had a rather ripe smell. The police were called and when they opened the trunk they found a dismembered body.

Some of the clothes had laundry marks which were traced to a Mrs Holt from Chelsea. When investigated it was discovered she was alive and her clothing had been stolen by a member of her staff.

She was asked to identify the head in the trunk. It was Annie Alice Bonati, who was known as Mrs Rolls.

The Southern Belle (was Greyhound Hotel), 175 & 177 Fulham Palace Road, W6 8QT
The police went to this, as his last known address and found a Mrs Robinson here, who was not John Robinson's only wife. She agreed to help the police find him. He was arrested when she received a call to meet him in the Elephant and Castle Pub in Walworth. He denied all knowledge of the murder.

The building is currently standing empty.

Old Bailey, EC4M 7EH
Robinson's trial started on July 11, 1927. As there was evidence to connect him to the murder he claimed he didn't intend to kill Minnie Bonati, and that when she became abusive to him he pushed her and thought he had just knocked her out. When he realised she was dead he panicked. The jury found him guilty.

Pentonville Prison, Caledonian Road, N7 8TT
He was hanged on August 12, 1927 at Pentonville.

Hawley Crescent Murder (1933)

30 Hawley Crescent, NW1 8QR

On the evening on January 3, 1933, Mr Wynne noticed that his shed in his back garden was on fire. When the fire brigade extinguished the fire, they discovered a burnt body inside.

The body was identified by a tenant as being that of Samuel Furnace. However, at the coroner's court, the judge examined the body and discovered a bullet wound in his back and the teeth were of a much younger man than Sam Furnace. Further examination of the body uncovered a Post Office book identifying him as 25-year-old Walter Spatchett who had been shot before being set on fire.

Sam Furnace who lived at Crogsland Road, left a note at his address which read; "Goodbye all. No work, no money, Sam J Furnace."

Crogsland Street has since been heavily refurbished and is unrecognisable.

The Hawley Crescent building is now Poppies fish and chip restaurant and has also been heavily re-constructed.

43 Dartmouth Park Road, Highgate, NW5 1SU

Walter Spatchett lived here with his parents and went missing two days before the fire.

Kentish Town Police Station, 10-12A Holmes Road, NW5 3AE

Furnace was arrested in Southend and brought to Kentish Town Police Station where he claimed that the shooting was accidental when he was 'showing' Walter the revolver. He claims he 'lost' his head and decided to burn the body.

He was put in a cell overnight, and complaining of the cold, he was given his overcoat back. He had some hydrochloric acid in his pocket which he took.

St Pancras Hospital, 4 Saint Pancras Way, Pancras Road, NW1 0PE

Samuel Furnace died 24 hours later on January 18 at St Pancras Hospital. He was later convicted of murder post-mortem.

The Casserley Murder (1938)

35 Lindesfarne Road, Wimbledon, SW20 0NW

Percy Arthur Casserly and his wife Georgina May (Ena) Casserley lived here in the late 1930s. They were married in 1927.

In the spring of 1937, the house next door to the Casserley's was being built and Mrs Casserley started an affair with the young foreman, Edward Royal Chaplin.

In September 1937, Ena Casserley discovered she was pregnant. Her husband was in a nursing home for his alcoholism but she wrote to him for a divorce. He refused.

He returned home on March 22, 1938. He was murdered the next day.

Ena had arranged to meet Edward, and they went to nearby Copse Hill. She told him she was afraid to go home, so he said, "you had better leave this to me," and returned home with her. She heard a scuffle between her lover and her husband and then two gunshots. Chaplin emerged unscathed.

Gap Road Cemetery, Gap Road, SW19 8JA

Percy Casserley was buried in the Gap Road Cemetery on the day that Chaplin was charged. Ena sent a wreath of red roses from "Sorrowing Ena."

Old Bailey, EC4M 7EH

Edward Chaplin and Ena Casserley's trial started in court No. 1 on May 24, 1938. His defence tried to use self-defence but the prosecution pointed out that Mr Casserley had been hit from behind and the bullet went through the back of his neck from a distance of more than 12 inches.

Chaplin was found guilty of manslaughter on May 27, 1939 and was sentenced to 12 years penal servitude. He served eight years.

Casserley, six months pregnant was sentenced to a nominal 11 days in prison and was released.

When Chaplin was released from prison, they got married.

Caxton Hall Murder (1940)

Caxton Hall, 8-10 Caxton Street, SW1H 0AQ

On March 13, 1940 there was a meeting at Caxton Hall of the East India Association and the Royal Central Asian Society. There were 160 people there to hear the lecture, 'Afghanistan the Present Position'.

When the meeting was wrapping up, Udham Singh (aka Singh Azad) walked down the aisle and shot six bullets onto the stage from his .45 Smith and Wesson revolver. The bullets however were .44 and were thirty years old. He was also carrying a knife.

Sir Michael O'Dwyer was shot twice in the back, Sir Louis Dane's arm was broken by a bullet, Lord Lamington injured his wrist and Lord Zetland, although shot twice survived.

Bow Street Police Station, 4 Bow Street, WC2E 7AT
Singh was arrested and taken to Bow Street Police Station where he said "Only one dead …eh? I thought I could get more."

Old Bailey, EC4M 7EH
His trial started at the Old Bailey on June 4, 1940, where he changed his story claiming he had planned to shoot into the ceiling in protest. After 95 minutes the jury found him guilty.

Pentonville Prison, Caledonian Road, N7 8TT
Singh was hanged on July 31, 1940 at Pentonville.

Elsham Road Murder (1941)

71a Elsham Road, West Kensington, W14 8HD
65-year-old Theodora Jessie Greenhill, a widow, had advertised in the autumn of 1941 for a lodger through a local estate agent.

On October 14, 1941 Harold Trevor, visited her and paid the deposit on the

Caxton Hall, 8-10 Caxton Street, SW1H 0AQ

71a Elsham Road, West Kensington, W14 8HD

Wandsworth Prison, Heathfield Road, SW18 3HU. Courtesy of geography.org.uk from Wikicommons Media

flat. As she was writing the receipt he hit her on the head with a beer bottle, knocking her out. He then strangled her and rifled through the flat looking for things to steal.

Trevor's big mistake was giving his real name to Mrs Greenhill, so when the police arrived the unfinished receipt bore the killer's name. Trevor was known to the police, as in the previous 40 years he had only been out of prison for eleven months.

Old Bailey, EC4M 7EH

Trevor was tried at the Old Bailey on January 28 and 29, 1942 where he was found guilty of murder.

Wandsworth Prison, Heathfield Road, SW18 3HU

He was hanged at Wandsworth prison on March 11, 1942.

Elizabeth McLindon (1946)

45 Chester Square, SW1W 9EA

In the 1940s this house was rented by King George II of Greece who had been exiled during the war. He employed a housekeeper, Elizabeth McLindon, who was a former prostitute. She was engaged to Arthur Boyce who had been instrumental in forging her references for the position. He was already married and had been in prison previously for bigamy and was wanted for cheque fraud.

On June 9, 1946, the king came to the property and was rather put out that there was no one there to greet him and the house hadn't been prepared. When the police broke into the servants' quarters they found Elizabeth dead, seated at the table, with a bullet wound to the back of the head.

Old Bailey, EC4M 7EH

Boyce had left some of his papers at the property amongst Elizabeth's things and he was arrested and tried at the Old Bailey. On the night of the murder she had confronted him about his wife and the cheque he had written to the jeweller for her engagement ring, which had bounced. Rather than be caught in another lie, he shot her dead.

He was found guilty of the murder and was hanged on November 1, 1947 at Pentonville prison.

Carnaby Street Shooting (1946)

Blue Lagoon, 50 Carnaby Street, W1F 9QF

Margaret Cook was killed outside the Blue Lagoon on Carnaby Street by a .25 bullet from a German automatic pistol on November 9, 1946. She had been in a borstal and was well-known to the police in the area and was working as a prostitute.

In 2015, a 91-year-old man confessed to the previously-unsolved murder and it is thought to be the longest period of time between a crime and a confession.

The unnamed man, who now lives in Canada, was apparently prompted to admit the crime following a cancer diagnosis.

Metropolitan Police detectives flew out to interview him, where he lives in a care home, and showed him pictures of 12 women, including Margaret, and he

Blue Lagoon, 50 Carnaby Street, W1F 9QF

successfully picked out his victim from the selection.

He said that he shot her with a WW2 Russian-made pistol after she cheated him out of money.

Newspaper reports from 1946, suggested her killer had been trying to take money from her. They also described a police chase of a man in a pork pie hat and Burberry-style raincoat in his mid to late twenties. The pursuit was unsuccessful, however, as the suspect vanished into the crowds.

He claims that five years later, he moved to the eastern Canadian province of Ontario, where he eventually became a citizen.

Today the club is Nobody's Child.

Margery Gardner (1946)

Abbey Court Hotel (was Pembridge Court Hotel), Pembridge Gardens, Notting Hill, W2 4DU

June 21, 1946, the body of a woman, Margery Gardner, was found on the bed at this address, murdered. She had been mutilated and bound.

She had been seen arriving at the hotel at around midnight with Neville Heath.

Nag's Head, 53 Kinnerton Street, Knightsbridge, SW1X 8ED

Margery Gardner was a regular here. She was working as a film extra as she waited for her art career to take off.

Neville Heath, who was dishonourably discharged from the RAF was calling himself Lieutenant Colonel Bill Armstrong of the South African Army and was also a regular here. He was seen drinking with Margery on the night of June 20.

The Nag's Head is open seven days a week for food and drink.

Old Bailey, EC4M 7EH

Heath was put on trial for the murder of Margery Gardner on September 24, 1946. He pleaded guilty on the grounds of insanity but the prosecution had

Nag's Head, 53 Kinnerton Street, Knightsbridge, SW1X 8ED

two doctors declare him sane. He was sentenced to death.

Pentonville Prison, Caledonian Road, N7 8TT

He was executed at Pentonville on October 16, 1946. He was offered a glass of whisky beforehand and he said, "Considering the circumstances, better make it a double."

Charlotte Street Robbery (1947)

J.S. Jays Jewellers, 73-75 Charlotte Street, W1T 4PL

On April 28, 1947 three masked men Charles Jenkins, 23, Christopher Geraghty,

MURDER | 83

J.S. Jays Jewellers, 73-75 Charlotte Street, W1T 4PL

20, and Terence Rolt, 17, attempted to rob the jewellers which once stood on this site. The current building is modern.

A shot was fired in the shop, and the assistant manager raised the alarm for the police. The gunmen fled the shop only to find their getaway car was blocked by a lorry. They ran towards Tottenham Court Road, where Alec de Antiquis drove his motorcycle in their path to block their escape. Chris Geraghty killed him by shooting him in the head.

It took three weeks to find the gunmen, all based on Charles Jenkins leaving his jacket at the scene. Both Geraghty and Jenkins were arrested and charged with murder.

Pentonville Prison, Caledonian Road, N7 8TT

Jenkins and Geraghty were hanged on September 19, 1947.

Covent Garden Murder (1948)

126 Long Acre, EC2E 9PE

On September 5, 1948 Helen Freedman/Freeman a Lithuanian prostitute, was found stabbed to death in her flat on Long Acre.

She was known as Russian Dora and had clearly fought for her life. Her flat was in a state of disarray, and there was a carving knife near her body bearing a fingerprint.

She was 56 but was able to make herself look much younger when she went out and had convinced a 26-year-old Canadian to propose although he changed his mind when he found out her age.

No one was ever arrested for the murder.

Ruth Ellis (1955)

The Little Club, 37 Brompton Road, SW3 1DE

Ruth Ellis worked here as a hostess as this exclusive club which entertained guests like King Hussein of Jordon, and actor Burt Lancaster.

Now it is a Dita clothes store.

The Little Club, 37 Brompton Road, SW3 1DE

Carroll's Club, 58 Duke Street, Mayfair, W1K 6JW

After leaving an abusive marriage, Ruth returned to work as a hostess at Carroll's. It was here she met racing driver David Blakely and fell hopelessly in love. She started to support him and let him move into her flat above the club. He was an alcoholic and violent towards her, with one attack resulting in a miscarriage.

29 Tanza Road, NW3 2UA

On Good Friday 1955, Blakely had failed to call Ruth, so she went to find him at a friend's house on Tanza Road. Seaton Findlater refused to let her in, but she could hear Blakely and the nanny inside. She was furious and smashed all the windows on his Standard Vanguard car.

Magdala Public House, South Hill Park, NW3 2SB

www.themagdala.co.uk

Carroll's Club, 58 Duke Street, Mayfair, W1K 6JW

Two days later, on Sunday evening Ruth followed Blakely to the Magdala where she waited for him to emerge. As he walked towards his car, she pulled the gun out. He glanced at her and then ignored her. She shot him at point blank range, and then when he was on the floor emptied the chamber into him.

Old Bailey, EC4M 7EH

Ruth was put on trial at the Old Bailey on June 20, 1955 to a packed public gallery. When asked what she thought would happen as she shot Blakely she answered, "I intended to kill him." The jury found her guilty within 14 minutes. She was sentenced to death.

Holloway Prison, Parkhurst Road, N7 0NU

On July 13, 1955 Ruth Ellis was hanged at Holloway prison. Such a group of protesters had gathered the police had to be called to control the 500-strong crowd. They had started gathering the day before calling for the death penalty to be lifted, with a petition signed by thousands including 35 members of London City Council. Ruth was the last woman to be hanged in England.

Holloway prison was closed in 2016.

St Mary's Church, Church Street, Old Amersham, HP7 0DB
www.stmaryschurchamersham.com

Ruth was originally buried in an unmarked grave in Holloway prison, but in the 1970s she was exhumed and reburied in the graveyard of St Mary's Church.

Although technically in Buckinghamshire, this churchyard is a 15-minute walk from Amersham underground station.

Cecil Court Murder (1961)

23 Cecil Court, WC2N 4EZ

On March 2, 1961, a scruffy young man came into Louis Meier's antique shop at 23 Cecil Court and asked about a dress sword and ornamental daggers that were for sale.

The next day, an apprentice sign maker came into the shop to buy a billiards cue. He saw what he thought was a dummy in the back room on the floor and ended up leaving the shop without investigating. When Mr Meier returned he found his assistant Elsie

23 Cecil Court, WC2N 4EZ

May Batten had been murdered with an ivory-handled dagger.

Bow Street Police Station, 4 Bow Street WC2E 7AH
Following descriptions of the youth given by Mr Meier and the owner of a local gun shop where the same youth had tried to sell a stolen sword from Mr Meier's store, Edwin Bush a 21-year-old Indian was arrested.

He took part in an identity parade at Bow Street Magistrates' where, he was clearly picked out of the line-up by the owner of the gun shop, although Mr Meier was less certain. With a palm print belonging to him found on the dagger, and a positive identity, Bush then confessed to the murder.

Old Bailey, EC4M 7EH
At his trial, which lasted only two days, Bush said Batten had been racist towards him when they were haggling over the price so he killed her in a rage. He was found guilty and sentenced to death.

Pentonville Prison, Caledonian Road, N7 8TT
He was the last person to be executed at Pentonville prison on July 6, 1961.

The Krays (1966)

Ronnie and Reggie Kray were twins born in the East End in 1933. They were talented boxers, but as they had been dishonourably discharged from National Service they were unable to go professional. Instead they turned to organised crime.

Blind Beggar Pub, 337 Whitechapel Road, E1 1BU
www.theblindbeggar.com

This was the location of the murder of George Cornell on March 10, 1966.

He was a member of a south London rival gang and had taunted Ronnie Kray about being homosexual in the past.

Cornell had come north of the river and was drinking in the Blind Beggar. Ronnie was in another pub when he heard Cornell was here. He entered the

Blind Beggar Pub, 337 Whitechapel Road, E1 1BU

Blind Beggar with John Barrie and shot Cornell through the eye.

Although the pub was busy, no one would bear witness to the crime as they were too afraid of the Krays.

The Carpenters Arms, 73 Cheshire Street, Bethnal Green, E2 6EG

This pub was bought by the Krays in 1967 for their mother Violet. They used it for various business meetings over the years, and on October 29, 1967 Reggie had a drink here before killing Jack McVitie.

97 Evering Road, Stoke Newington, N16 7SJ

On October 29, 1967 Jack 'The Hat' McVitie, was invited to a party in Blonde Carol's flat in Stoke Newington, and was promised 'party, birds and booze.' The party was in the basement flat of 97 Evering Road. The Krays got there first and removed all the other guests.

When McVitie arrived, Reggie Kray attempted to shoot him, but the gun jammed and instead stabbed him in the face, chest and stomach numerous times.

St Mary's Church, Saint Marychurch Street, SE16 4NF

The body of Jack 'The Hat' was dumped outside the church, although it was quickly moved before the police got to it.

The brothers and their gang were arrested.

Tate Modern, Bankside, SE1 9TG

The body of McVitie was never found and Ronnie over the years has said it was fed to the pigs in Suffolk, buried beneath a city office block or burnt in the furnaces at the Bankside Power Station, which is now the Tate Modern.

43 Braithwaite House, St Luke's, EC1Y 8NE

On May 8, 1968 Ronnie and Reggie were arrested in connection with gangland crimes including murder and fraud in their mother's flat in this block of 1960s brutalist architecture.

Old Bailey, EC4M 7EH

On March 4, 1969, Reggie and Ronnie Kray were found guilty at their trial at the Old Bailey; Reggie of murdering Jack McVitie, and Ronnie of murdering George Cornell. They were sentenced to life imprisonment, with a minimum of 30 years each.

It was the Old Bailey's longest and most expensive trial at 39 days. The jury took six hours and 55 minutes to come to a verdict.

Chingford Mount Cemetery, 121 Old Church Road, E4 6ST

Ronnie died in March 1995 in prison, and Reggie was allowed parole early as he was suffering from inoperable cancer in 2000. He died within a month on October 1, 2000. They are buried alongside their brother Charlie Kray who also died in 2000, their

Tate Modern, Bankside, SE1 9TG

mother Violet and father Charlie, Reggie's wife Frances and Charlie Jnr's son Gary.

To find the graves, from the entrance walk down North Way towards the top left-hand corner of the cemetery. They are buried on the corner of Memorial Way and Remembrance Walk.

Massacre of Braybrook Street (1966)

Shepherd's Bush Police Station, 252 Uxbridge Road, W12 7JA

On August 12, 1966, PC Roger Fox, PC Wombwell, PS Head all left the station in an unmarked Triumph Q-car police car to start their shift.

At the time of writing the police station has been permanently closed and was standing derelict.

Marylebone Magistrates' Court, 181 Marylebone Road, NW1 5BR

The three policemen dropped off DI Coote at the magistrates' court where he was giving evidence against five men who had escaped from Wormwood Scrubs prison.

East Acton Police Station, W12 0BP

At 3:10 on August 12, 1966 a blue Vanguard left the car park with John

Shepherd's Bush Police Station, 252 Uxbridge Road, W12 7JA

Marylebone Magistrates' Court, 181 Marylebone Road, NW1 5BR

Edward Witney driving, Harry Roberts and John Duddy were passengers, and there was a bag with false number plates, a mask, some overalls and three guns in the front of the car. They were looking to steal a car.

Wymering Mansions, 181 Wymering Road, Maida Vale, W9 2NQ

Harry Maurice Roberts lived here with Lilian Margaret Perry and another couple, the Howards and their three children.

Basement Flat, 10 Fernhead Road, Maida Vale, W9 3ET

John Witney lived here with his wife. After searching the flat, the police found no weapons or anything illegal.

[59] Braybrook Street, W12 0AS

The Vanguard car entered Braybook Street and had attracted the attention of the police car who flagged them down. PC Wombwell and PS Head approached the driver's window. Head asked Witney for his road fund license,

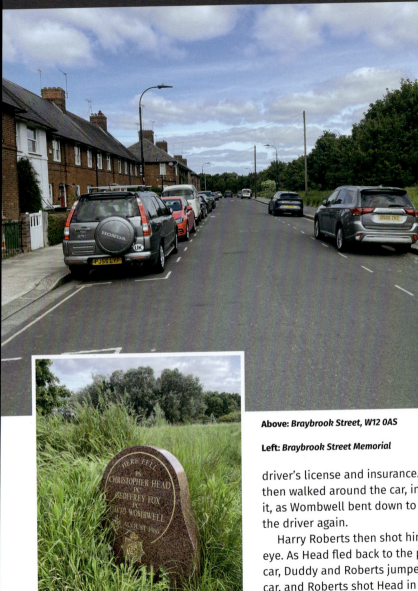

Above: *Braybrook Street, W12 0AS*

Left: *Braybrook Street Memorial*

driver's license and insurance. Head then walked around the car, inspecting it, as Wombwell bent down to speak to the driver again.

Harry Roberts then shot him in the eye. As Head fled back to the police car, Duddy and Roberts jumped out the car, and Roberts shot Head in the back. Duddy then shot at Fox in the driver's seat of the police car hitting him in the head.

103 Railway Arch Tinworth Street, Vauxhall, SE11 5EQ

Witney left the Vanguard car in a lockup under the railway arches of the main railway line to Waterloo on Tinworth Street.

Parish Church of St Stephen and St Thomas, 1 Coverdale Road, W12 8JJ

August 31, 1966 the three policemen were buried following a ceremony in this church. There were 600 policemen on the route of the funeral procession.

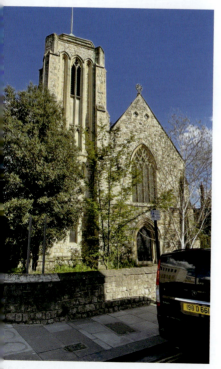

Parish Church of St Stephen and St Thomas, 1 Coverdale Road, W12 8JJ

Old Bailey, EC4M 7EH

The trial of Duddy, Roberts and Witney began at the Old Bailey on December 6, 1966. Witney and Duddy pleaded not guilty, Roberts pleaded guilty to the murders of Head and Wombwell and not guilty to the murder of Fox but guilty as an accessory to murder. They were all found guilty of murder and processing firearms, and each sentenced to thirty years in prison.

Lord Lucan (1974)

46 Lower Belgrave Street, SW1W 0LN

On Thursday, November 7, 1974 Sandra Rivett was murdered at this address. The house belonged to Richard John Bingham, 7th Earl of Lucan, more commonly known as Lord Lucan and his wife Veronica Mary Duncan.

On the night of the murder Sandra, the nanny was not meant to be working, and had planned to spend the night at her boyfriend's house. She put the children to bed at about 8:55pm and offered to make Veronica a cup of tea. She headed to the basement kitchen where an assailant was waiting and bludgeoned her to death.

Veronica came down the stairs to see what had happened to the tea when Sandra had not returned and was also attacked and hit over the head. Veronica later identified the assailant as her husband and while he washed himself in the family bathroom, she made her escape.

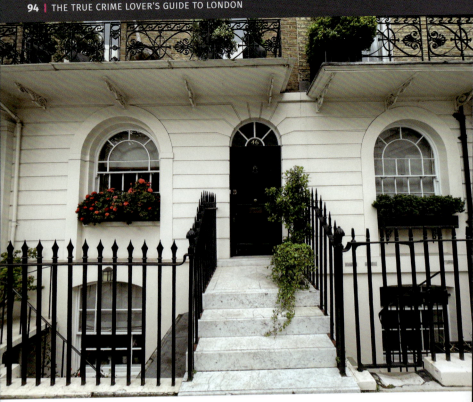

Above: *46 Lower Belgrave Street, SW1W 0LN*

Below: *Plumbers Arms, 14 Lower Belgrave Street, SW1W 0LN*

Plumbers Arms, 14 Lower Belgrave Street, SW1W 0LN
www.greeneking.co.uk/pubs/greater-london/plumbers-arms

On the night of the murder, Veronica fled the house and headed to the Plumbers Arms to raise the alarm.

At the inquest into Rivett's death, held in June 1975, the jury returned a verdict naming Lucan as her killer.

5 Eaton Row, SW1W 0JA
This property was owned by Veronica, but Lord Lucan often spent nights here before the marriage broke down in 1973.

72a Elizabeth Street, SW1W 9PD
In 1972, Lord Lucan had separated from his wife so he wasn't living in the Lower Belgrave Street address at the time of the murder and instead was staying here in a ground floor flat.

Clermont Club, 44 Berkeley Square, W1J 5AR
Lord Lucan spent much of his free time at John Aspinall's Clermont Club, where he engaged in his gambling habit.

The club was opened in 1962 by John Aspinall and Lord Lucan was one of the original members. In

Eaton Row, SW1W 0JA

72a Elizabeth Street, SW1W 9PD

Clermont Club, 44 Berkeley Square, W1J 5AR

1972, Aspinall sold it to the Playboy Club and Lucan hated how members of the Playboy Club could come to the Clermont and 'dilute the exclusivity'. The club closed in 1982.

St George's Hospital, Blackshaw Road, SW17 0QT

After reporting the murder to the police, Veronica was taken to St George's Hospital where she was treated for her head wounds.

51 Chester Square, SW1W 9EA

Following the murder, blood was found on the doorstep of Madeleine Florman's home. She was a friend of Lucan and at 10pm, was woken by the doorbell. She didn't answer the bell and later received an agitated call from Lucan before he hung up. Later he called his mother and visited a friend in East Sussex. He was never seen again.

Bow Street Magistrates' Court, 4 Bow Street WC2E 7AH

On November 8, 1974 warrants for Lord Lucan's arrest were issued and detectives were placed at homes connected to him and his friends in Europe, USA and the West Indies. He has never been found.

51 Chester Square, SW1W 9EA

8

SERIAL KILLERS

London has seen a lot of serial killers over the decades. A serial killer is defined as someone who has killed more than three people over a period of time, even if they have cooling off periods in between. Generally the method of killing, and the motives remain the same across all murders. There is often little to no contact between the victim and murderer and often the motivation is sadistic or sexual. They generally continue killing until they are caught, imprisoned or die.

The Deptford Poisonings (1885-89)

Amelia Winters (née Goodman) is the only known female serial killer in London. Between 1885 and 1888 the insurance company Liverpool Victoria Friendly Society accepted insurance payments from Amelia for 22 people aged between nine and 73, including family members and lodgers. It was possible to insure the lives of individuals without their knowledge at this time.

Mrs Winters paid Liverpool Victoria Friendly Society 7s 6d per week and the policies totalled £240. The company paid out £45 12s, with no distrust or suspicion.

She also took out thirteen policies from April 28, 1884 to January 14, 1889 with the Prudential Assurance Company.

At least six people fell victim to Winters: Benjamin Winters, William Winters, Anna Bolton, Elizabeth Frost, Sidney Bolton and William Sutton. Her daughter Elizabeth was charged with the murder of three people but Amelia confessed to the murders on her deathbed, meaning Elizabeth was only found guilty of forgery.

St Nicholas' Church, Deptford Green, SE8 3DQ

Amelia married Joseph Winters, on January 29, 1854 at St Nicholas' Church. They went on to have at least five children.

Friendly Street, Deptford, SE8 4DT

Anna Bolton (née Goodman), aged 63, Amelia's older sister, died on Friendly Street in November 1886. Amelia had taken insurance out on her in March for £3 and collected the pay-out of £1 10s upon her death.

Brockley Cemetery, 113 Brockley Grove, SE4 1DZ

Elizabeth Jane Frost was buried here following her death on February 8, 1888. Her son Thomas had married Elizabeth Winters, Amelia's daughter. Mrs Frost had been taken ill on February 2 following a visit to the Winters, and she was unable to keep anything down. On September 26, 1885, a policy on the life of Elizabeth Jane Frost for £9 9s was made by Amelia Winters, and £8 5s in gold was paid to Amelia on her death on February 8.

Elizabeth Jane Frost was exhumed on June 15, 1889 and her body showed signs of arsenic poisoning.

William Sutton was buried here following his death on December 10, 1888. He had gone to stay with Amelia after leaving the workhouse. He was healthy when he was at the workhouse but not long after he came to her on December 4, 1888 he was taken ill. He was dead six days later.

Amelia Winters collected insurance of £8 14s on December 11. There had been two policies on his life, and one had been recently increased. On May 14, 1869, in the early morning, acting under a Home Office warrant, Sutton's body was exhumed and showed signs of arsenic poisoning.

Sidney Bolton was buried here on February 16, 1889 and his body also showed signs of arsenic poisoning. Amelia had looked after James Bolton's two children Sidney and Mary, whilst he was at work. He rented rooms from her daughter Elizabeth. Amelia had taken insurance out on his life and the two children for £5 each in January 1889. The premiums on the latter were increased in October.

Mary was taken ill in November 1888, with vomiting which was to last for nine weeks. Amelia Winters nursed her. Mary was lucky and recovered. After Christmas 1888, Sidney became ill and by the end of January the doctor said there was nothing more he could do for the boy. He died on February 11, 1889. Amelia received £20 payment from Liverpool Victoria Insurance Company.

Amelia Winters was buried here on July 22, 1889 in consecrated ground. Only her widower, his sons and the officials were present. She died on July 14, 1889 aged 59, before she could be charged. She was recorded as dying of marasmus or general wasting.

Amelia's (unmarked) grave was under two lime trees, between the cemetery wall and a footpath, near the graves of Bolton, Sutton and Mrs Frost.

Brockley Barge (was The Breakspeare Arms), 184 Brockley Road, SE4 2RR

www.jdwetherspoon.com/pub-histories/england/london/the-brockley-barge-brockley

On April 18, 1889, the inquest into the death of Sidney Bolton was started at the Breakspeare Arms, and then on June 1 following the exhumation of

William Sutton it was resumed on July 9. Amelia Winters was unable to attend due to ill health.

Until the 1990s the pub was called the Breakspeare Arms. It was then closed due to getting a bad reputation for violence and drugs. Now it is a Wetherspoons and has been rebranded as the Brockley Barge.

5 Creak Street, Deptford, SE8 3BT

Amelia's nephew James Samuel Bolton lived here in 1888. He paid her to look after his children, not realising one then the other would become sick and he would lose his son Sidney.

Old Bailey, EC4M 7EH

Elizabeth Frost, Amelia's daughter, was put on trial for forgery on July 29, 1889 and for three murders on October 21: William Sutton, Sidney Bolton and Elizabeth Frost her mother-in-law. She pleaded not guilty.

The jury found her not guilty of murder as her mother had exonerated her on her death bed, but she got seven years for forgery and was sent to Woking Female Prison at Knaphill to serve her sentence.

Whitechapel Murders (1888)

The name Jack the Ripper came from a letter sent to the Central News Agency on September 27, 1888. The letter may have been a hoax but the press ran with the name and it has led to most serial killers having the epithet of Ripper ever since.

There were officially five victims of Jack the Ripper: Mary Ann Nichols, Annie Chapman, Elizabeth Stride, Catherine Eddowes and Mary Jane Kelly. However, there could be as many as eleven victims who all bear similar wounds.

The majority of the Whitechapel area has been refurbished since, so there are very few sites remaining.

1 Brick Lane, E1 7SA

Emma Smith, a prostitute, was brutally attacked on Tuesday April 3, 1888 near the Taylor's cocoa factory which stood on the corner of Brick Lane and Wentworth Street. The factory has since been replaced with 1 Brick Lane, a tall tower block. Three men, including a youth, attacked her and she died from her injuries the next day.

Some people believe she could have been one of the earlier victims.

Osborn Street, E1 6TD

Mary Ann Nichols was last seen walking down this street at 2:30am on August 31, 1888 by Emily Holland. They had had a conversation about needing to earn her doss money as she had spent it all on alcohol.

Ye Frying Pan Pub, 16 Brick Lane, E1 6PU

This Indian restaurant (Shaad) used to be the Ye Frying Pan Pub, and was where the first victim, Mary Ann 'Polly'

1 Brick Lane, E1 7SA

Ye Frying Pan Pub, 16 Brick Lane, E1 6PU

Nichols was drinking before she was murdered on August 31, 1888. She left the pub at 2:30am after she had spent all her money. Within the hour she was dead.

If you look up to the top of the building you will see the old, engraved pub sign.

Thrawl Street, E1 6RT

Mary Ann Nichols had lodgings in Thrawl Street, just alongside Ye Frying Pan, at the time of her murder. Frances Coles, also lived in a women's only lodging house on Thrawl Street in 1891, shortly before her murder.

Working Lad's Institute, 283 Whitechapel Road, E1 1BY

The inquest for Mary Ann Nichols' death was held in the Working Lad's Institute on Saturday, September 1, 1888.

The institute building is the tall orange brick structure next to Whitechapel Underground Station.

29 Hanbury Street, Spitalfields, E1 6QR

On Saturday September 8, 1888, Annie Chapman (née Smith), aged 47, was discovered near the steps to the doorway of the back yard of 29 Hanbury Street. She had been thrown out of a doss house at 2am and had nowhere to

go, so was walking the streets when she came across Jack. Her possessions had been lain at her feet including two brass rings, a few pennies and two farthings.

The buildings on the opposite side of the road give an idea of what it would have looked like, but number 29 is a modern building.

35 Dorset Street, W1U 6QR
www.barleymowlondon.co.uk

Annie Chapman was staying at a lodging house at number 35 which was run by Timothy Donovan. She arrived at midnight of September 7, 1888, drunk. She told Tim to hold the bed for her as she was short of the rent and therefore went out again at about 1:50am.

The building houses the Barley Mow Pub which was established in 1791.

Henriques Street (was Dutfield's Yard, off Berner Street), E1 1NT
Jack's third victim, Elizabeth Stride, was discovered in Dutfield's Yard or Berner Street which is now Henriques Street on Sunday September 30, 1888.

Born near Gothenburg in Sweden, Elizabeth was 44 when she died. She had some flowers pinned to her dress as she looked for customers. Elizabeth was then seen outside 58 Berner Street with a man talking at 11:45pm on the night she died.

Jack had been disturbed whilst killing her and went on to kill another on the same night.

35 Dorset Street, W1U 6QR

Dutfield's yard was between 40 and 42 Berner Street. The buildings on either side of the road were cleared for the Harry Gosling Primary School.

Queen's Head Pub, 74 Commercial Street, E1 6LY
On Saturday September 29, 1888, Elizabeth Stride went to this pub with her landlady, Elizabeth Tanner. It was the last time Tanner saw her alive.

They returned to the lodging house together. She was seen by a

Queen's Head Pub, 74 Commercial Street, E1 6LY

charwoman, Catherine Lane, at the lodgings between 6-7pm that evening.

Now this is Pangea Café.

29 Aldgate High Street, EC3N 1DL

At 8:30pm on September 29, 1888 Catherine Eddowes was picked up outside number 29 by the police for being drunk - so drunk she was unable to walk by herself. She was taken to Bishopsgate Police Station and was released at about 12:30am on September 30, 1888.

No 29 is now a glass office block.

Mitre Square, EC3A 5DE

The second victim on Sunday September 30, 1888, and Jack's fourth victim was Catherine Eddowes.

She was discovered lying in Mitre Square. She had spent the evening in a police cell at Bishopsgate Police Station and had been released at 12:30am. It wasn't long until her body was discovered.

Her body was taken to The City of London Mortuary and Coroner's Court, Golden Lane, EC1Y 0QT. The original building was damaged in the Second World War and has since been replaced.

Ten Bells Pub, 84 Commercial Street, E1 6QQ

www.tenbells.com

On the night of November 8, 1888, Mary Kelly stopped off at the Ten Bells pub, which was her 'patch' for picking up punters in order to pay the rent.

Mary was the only victim found inside and was discovered in 13 Miller's Court off Dorset Street, E1. As her murder happened inside, Jack had spent more time, and hers was the most gruesome of the victims. Miller's Court and Dorset Street have been completely reconfigured since 1888, and there is no longer anything of the original layout left.

In the 1930s the landlady, Annie Chapman, had renamed the pub Jack the Ripper, but it has since returned to the original name and retains a number of original features.

The pub is open seven days a week.

Ten Bells Pub, 84 Commercial Street, E1 6QQ

Lilian Knowles House (was Providence Row Refuge), 50 Crispin Street, E1 6HQ

Before Mary Kelly turned to prostitution she had stayed at the Providence Row Refuge. They helped her find a job as a domestic servant before she moved out to make her own way. The job didn't work out and she ended up as a sex-worker on the streets of Whitechapel.

Shoreditch Town Hall, 380 Old Street, EC1V 9LT

The inquest of Mary Kelly took place here on November 12, 1888.

The building is now a performing arts theatre.

Old Castle Street (was Castle Alley), Whitechapel, E6 1PP

Alice McKenzie was discovered in Castle Alley on July 17, 1889 and is thought by some to be a Ripper victim although her killer appeared to be left-handed, whereas the Ripper was right-handed.

She left her digs in Gun Street and was last seen alive at 11:40pm in Brick Lane.

Her throat had been cut and there were stab wounds on her abdomen. She was murdered between 12:30 and 12:45am. Her body was found just past the wash houses on the same side of the street, under a streetlamp.

Lilian Knowles House (was Providence Row Refuge), 50 Crispin Street, E1 6HQ

This building is particularly interesting as it is just the façade of the original wash house with a completely new building behind.

Pinchin Street, E1 1SA

A female torso was found under a railway arch in Pinchin Street, in the early hours of the morning of September 11, 1889. As the site was close to Berner Street where Elizabeth Stride was discovered some thought it could also have been the work of Ripper, although the *modus operandi* was different.

Happy Days Chip Shop, 44/46 Goulston Street, E1 7TP

In 1891 the window to the left of the chip shop was a doorway leading to a staircase which took you into the flats above.

These flats were primarily inhabited by the Jewish community. It was inside this doorway that the piece of blood-soaked apron thought to belong to Catherine Eddowes, as well as the graffiti on the wall which read: "The Juwes are the men that will not be blamed for nothing." The police wiped it off before it was photographed in case it caused problems for the residents.

45 Chamber Street, E1 8BL

In 1891 the railway arches on Chamber Street were open allowing passage through to the other side.

The body of Frances Coles was found under the last arch on this road at 2:15am on February 13. She was still alive when the police found her, which prevented him from following the footsteps they could hear running away from the site. Her throat had been cut twice and she died shortly afterwards.

James Sadler was arrested for the murder but was released on March 3 due to lack of evidence. Some think she may have been another Jack the Ripper victim.

Happy Days Chip Shop, 44/46 Goulston Street, E1 7TP

Culpeper Pub (was Princess Alice Pub), 40 Commercial Street, E1 6TB

Culpeper Pub (was Princess Alice), 40 Commercial Street, E1 6TB
www.theculpeper.com

Frances Coles came to the Princess Alice on February 11, 1891 and met up with James Sadler, an old client of hers. They spent three days and two nights together and he bought her a new hat.

The top floor has recently been added and there is a roof garden. They are open seven days a week for food and drink.

8 Whites Row (was Spitalfields Chambers), E1 7NF
Frances Coles and James Sadler stayed at a building on this site from February 11, 1891. They were thrown out for not having the money for the night's stay on February 13, the night she was murdered.

The building on the site isn't the original but is on the footprint of the lodging house.

Manor Park Cemetery, Sebert Road, Forest Gate, E7 0NP
Mary Ann Chapman, aged 47, was the second victim of Jack the Ripper. She is buried in Manor Park Cemetery. She came to London from Windsor in the 1880s, and made a living through prostitution, selling artificial flowers and needlework. There is a small plaque marking the grave.

8 Whites Row (was Spitalfields Chambers), E1 7NF

East London Cemetery, Grange Road, E13 0HB
Two of Jack the Ripper's victims are buried in East London Cemetery: Elizabeth Stride and Frances Coles. Another possible victim was Alice McKenzie, aged 44, from Peterborough. She had the nickname Clay Pipe Alice and was also buried here.

Elizabeth was buried in a pauper's grave, which has since been upgraded with a marble surround. To find the grave, walk towards the war memorial, and turn left along the path. Then follow the main path to the right, and then bear left along a gravel path. Elizabeth was 45 when she was murdered and had turned to prostitution when her marriage broke down.

Frances Coles was the last of the victims of Jack the Ripper and was murdered in 1891. She was 29 (31 according to Find a Grave) and known as Carroty Nell because of her red hair. The night before she died she had just obtained a new black silk bonnet.

Walthamstow (St Patrick's) Roman Catholic Cemetery, Queen's Road, E17 8QP

Mary Jane Kelly the fifth victim was buried in St Patrick's Roman Catholic Cemetery. She was only 25 when she was murdered and had been in London for four years where she moved to live with a cousin. She was Irish, from Limerick but had grown up in Caernarvonshire in Wales. In London she lived with a Billingsgate fish porter but she slipped into prostitution. Her obituary announced that "no family member could be found to attend the funeral" but due to the horrific nature of her death her funeral had hundreds of attendees.

The exact location of her burial isn't known, but there is a marker in what is thought to be the approximate spot. When you walk through the gates of the cemetery, keep to the left of the chapel building, walk past the large McCarthy family grave, and turn left on the path. As you walk down the path you will see a statue of a footballer, and Mary's marker is just behind that.

City of London Cemetery, Aldersbrook Road, E12 5DQ

Mary Ann Nichols, the first Ripper victim was buried at City of London Cemetery, in an unmarked grave but there is a plaque commemorating her. To find her plaque head towards the red-roofed traditional crematorium, walk anti-clockwise around the crematorium and walk along the path until you pass the pond on your right. Turn left on Memorial Way and keep walking until you find the marker. She was 42 when she died. Her father Edward Walker was at the funeral with two of her children.

The commemorative plaque to the fourth victim, Catherine Eddowes, can be found a little further along the path. She was originally buried in an unmarked pauper's grave. She was 46 when she was murdered and left behind three children.

The Lambeth Poisonings (1891-92)

Dr Thomas Neill Cream, a Canadian doctor, committed a number of murders by administering strychnine to prostitutes and leaving them to die alone. He then wrote a number of blackmail letters to eminent people claiming to have evidence which proved

SERIAL KILLERS | 111

their roles in the murders. These letters were passed onto the police and money not paid. His handwriting was eventually matched with these letters.

Following Cream's execution, it was discovered his wife in Canada had died in 1877 in mysterious circumstances, and in 1879 a woman's body was found in his practice in Ontario. This led to a quick move of practice to Chicago where Julia Faulkner died in 1880 following an abortion carried out by Cream.

Although arrested in Canada, Cream was acquitted for murder. In 1881 he was convicted of the murder of the husband of a woman he was having an affair with, but this was commuted and concluded, meaning he was released in 1888.

8 Duke Street, St James's, SW1Y 6BL
Ellen Donworth, a 19-year-old, prostitute lived here with Ernest Lennett. On the evening of October 13, 1891 she told Lennett she was going to see her mother, but instead went to Morpeth Place, where she was seen entering a house with various men.

St Thomas' Hospital, Westminster Bridge Road, SE1 7EH
Ellen was found collapsed on Morpeth Road, at about 7:45pm on October 13. She said a man on the street had given her something white to drink. She was taken to St Thomas' Hospital where she died later that evening. There were traces of strychnine and morphia in her stomach.

Another victim Alice Marsh died on the way to St Thomas' Hospital on April 13, 1892, and Emma Shrivell two hours after her arrival at the hospital, having given a statement to the police in the cab. There was evidence of large amounts strychnine in the stomachs of both women.

27 Lambeth Road, SE1 7DG
Matilda Clover (aka Phillips), 27, lived in two rooms on the second floor here with her young child. She was "living a loose life" and tended to drink heavily. On the evening of October 20, 1891 she was seen returning home with a tall man wearing a silk top hat.

She popped out to get two beers and spent another hour with him before he left. At 3am she woke, screaming in pain. She died at 9am on October 21, 1891. The doctor assumed it was due to excessive drinking and the police weren't informed. Her body was exhumed on May 5, 1892 once the connection had been made, and the post-mortem showed strychnine poisoning.

Tooting Cemetery, Blackshaw Road, Tooting, SW17 0BY
Matilda Clover was buried here on October 27.

44 Townshend Road, St John's Wood, NW8 6LE
Louisa Harris aka Loo Harvey, lived here with Charles Harvey, a bus driver.

Northumberland Arms Pub, 119 Tottenham Court Road, W1T 5AW

www.greatukpubs.co.uk/ northumberland-arms-bloomsbury

On October 21, 1891, Loo Harvey was at Alhambra Music Hall and met a man after the show on Regent Street. They went to a hotel on Berwick Street.

He claimed to be a doctor from St Thomas's and said he could cure her of some spots on her forehead with some pills. She arranged to meet him the next day.

They went to the Northumberland Arms pub for some wine where he gave her the pills and arranged to meet her later. She pretended to take them but instead threw them away.

He didn't show up to their later rendezvous. She bumped into him again a month later, but he denied all knowledge and seemed annoyed about the situation.

118 Stamford Street, Blackfriars, SE1 9NN

Alice Marsh and Emma Shrivell lived at 118 Stamford Street where the landlady allowed them to have gentlemen visitors.

On April 12, 1892, a policeman saw a man leaving the property, and then in the early hours of April 13 both Alice and Emma were screaming in agony. They told the police that a man who claimed to be a doctor had given them both three long pills.

103 Lambeth Palace Road, SE1 7LG

Dr Thomas Cream lived at this address in October 1891. He claimed he was fascinated with the recent poisonings and tried to discuss the case with his landlady's daughter Emily Sleaper.

He told her that another lodger, Dr Harper, was the murderer. He further discussed the case with other associates.

He approached the police about being persecuted by the police, and when the detective came to talk to him they discovered a large jar of strychnine pills. Once his handwriting had been matched with the letters he was arrested on June 3, 1892.

Bow Street Police Station, 4 Bow Street, WC2E 7AT

After his arrest, Dr Thomas Neill Cream was brought here and charged. He took part in an identity parade where housemates Elizabeth May and Elizabeth Masters picked him out of a line-up of 20 people. They had let Matilda Clover back into their lodgings and had seen the man she was with before she died.

Old Bailey, EC4M 7EH

Dr Thomas Neill Cream was sent to trial at the Old Bailey which started on October 17, 1892. He was charged with four murders: Ellen Donworth, Matilda Clover, Alice Marsh, Emma Shrivell the attempted murder of Louisa Harris and attempting to extort money. He pleaded not guilty.

The jury took 10 minutes to find him guilty and he was sentenced to death.

*Northumberland Arms Pub,
119 Tottenham Court Road, W1T 5AW*

SERIAL KILLERS | 113

He was sent to Newgate Prison, next door to the Old Bailey.

His execution took place on November 15, 1892.

George Chapman (1897-1903)

George Chapman was born as Sewerin Antoniovich Klosowski in Poland in December 1865. In Poland he received medical training, although he was not a qualified doctor, being the equivalent of a paramedic today.

When living in Hastings in April 1897 he bought an ounce of tartar emetic, and 146 ounces of antimony. Only two ounces of antimony can be fatal.

His three wives, Mary Spink, Bessie Taylor and Maud Marsh all had evidence of antinomy in their stomachs in fatal quantities. He never gave a reason why he killed his wives, and there was no clear motive.

7 Church Lane, Bushwood, E11 1HG

George was working here as a hairdresser's assistant when he met Mary Isabella Renton (Spink) as they both lived in the same lodgings in Forest Road, Leytonstone.

They announced to the landlady they were now married, although they were both already married to living spouses. On October 29, 1889 Chapman had married Lucy Baderska, and had one son, Wladyslaw, on September 6, 1890 and a daughter, Cecilia, born on May 12, 1892. Wladyslaw died on

March 3, 1891, and Cecilia lived until 1960. Chapman and Baderska split up before 1893 but didn't divorce.

Prince of Wales, 20 Bartholomew Square, EC1V 3QT

After returning to London from Hastings in September 1897, Chapman took the license of the Prince of Wales Pub. His wife Mary Spink was beginning to look thin and unwell, and she was said to vomit most nights. Mary died here on Christmas Day 1897.

In March 1898, Chapman advertised for a barmaid, to which Bessie Taylor applied. She was a couple of years older than him but had never been married and didn't have any children. They were 'married' at Easter 1898.

This pub is now an interior designers called Rients Ltd.

St Patrick's Roman Catholic Cemetery, Langthorne Road, E11 4HL

Mary Spink was buried in St Patrick's on December 30, 1897, in a common grave without a headstone. Her body was exhumed for post-mortem on December 9, 1902.

Monument Pub, 135 Union Street, Southwark, SE1 0FA

Returning to London from Hertfordshire, George and Bessie took over the license of the Monument Pub in March 1900. In December of that year, she started suffering with abdominal pains, vomiting and diarrhoea. She first saw a doctor on January 1, 1901 and she died here on February 13, 1901.

In August 1901 Chapman advertised for a barmaid and Maud Eliza Marsh, aged 19, applied. They 'married' in October 1901.

On October 25, the Monument caught fire, and although Chapman didn't gain financially many thought he had torched the place.

It was never rebuilt and was replaced with a modern office building.

The Crown, 213 Borough High Street, SE1 1JA

From November 11, 1901 Chapman took over The Crown, with Maud by his side.

She died here on October 22, 1902 following a long illness where the Marsh family doctor from Croydon thought she had been poisoned with arsenic.

The doctor was suspicious and insisted on carrying out a post-mortem. Traces of arsenic were found in her stomach as well as antinomy.

On October 25, 1902, the police went to The Crown to speak to George Chapman about poisoning his wife. He was arrested later that day. Now a derelict building but if you look up you can still see the crown moulding.

Guy's Hospital, Great Maze Pond, SE1 9RT

Maud fell violently ill from July 28, 1902 to August 20 and was staying at Guy's Hospital. When she returned home she fell ill again in October.

Southwark Magistrates' Court, 1 English Grounds, SE1 2HU

On October 27, 1902, George Chapman was charged with the murder of Maud Marsh.

By February 1903 he had been seen at the magistrates' court 17 times in regard to the murder of his three wives.

Old Bailey, EC4M 7EH

Chapman was sent for trial at the Old Bailey on March 16, 1903. The trial lasted four days and the jury returned a guilty verdict within 10 minutes.

Wandsworth Prison, Heathfield Road, SW18 3HU

George Chapman was hanged for the murder of Maud Marsh on April 7, 1903. Many thought he could be Jack the Ripper, but no evidence came forward. He was buried in the Wandsworth Prison cemetery.

In his will he left £15,000 equivalent to the family of Bessie Taylor but only a ring and some clothing for Maud Marsh's family.

The Brides in the Bath (1912-14)

George Joseph Smith was married to Edith Peglar in Bristol, but as a means of making money he 'married' other women under pseudonyms across the country, resulting in two murders in the bath before he came to London.

He convinced his wives to sign over all their wealth to him, to write a will in his favour as well as taking out life insurance. Then he took them to the doctor complaining they were ill and susceptible to seizures and headaches, although rarely did they speak to the doctor directly.

In total he married eight women and killed three of them, one in London: Beatrice "Bessie" Mundy, July 12, 1912 in Blackpool; Alice Smith (née Burnham) December 1913, in Bath and Margaret Elizabeth Lloyd (née Lofty), 38, December 18, 1914 in London.

It was only when the London death made the papers that relatives of the other two victims sent news clippings to the police to show the similarities in the cases.

92 Roman Road, Bethnal Green, E6 3SR

George Smith was born in this house on January 11, 1872.

National Gallery, Trafalgar Square, WC2N 5DN

In October 1909, Smith married Sarah Freeman from Southampton. He had emptied her Post Office account and she had sold some government stock shortly after they were married. On November 5, he took her to the National Gallery.

He popped to the toilet while she waited inside. He never returned. Instead he returned to their home and stole all of her belongings leaving her destitute. She never saw him again.

369 Brixton Road, SW9 7DE

On December 18, 1913 Smith went to the solicitors here (Kingsbury and Turners) following the death of his wife Alice Burnham in the bathtub in Blackpool. He showed them the will of his late wife and the insurance policy on her life. It amounted to £604 less fees and probate was granted on December 29.

Woolwich Registry Office, Town Hall, Wellington Street, SE18 6PW

George Smith met Alice Reavil, 42, in Bournemouth and they were married in Woolwich on September 17, 1914. She withdrew all her savings and gave the money to her new husband (£76 6s). On September 22 he went for a walk in Brockwell Park and never returned, having taken her money and clothes. She died a spinster in 1959.

31 Archway Road, N19 3TU

George Smith took his wife Margaret Elizabeth Lofty to Dr Stephen Bates at this address for a check-up as he claimed she was suffering from a headache. She was unable to answer any of the doctor's questions. This was a pattern which Smith had followed twice before as a means of sowing the seeds of an illness.

16 Orchard Road, Highgate, N6 5TR

George Smith rented rooms here after insisting there was a bath available. He thought it was rather small but paid a deposit of six shillings. On

369 Brixton Road, SW9 7DE

December 14, 1914 he returned with his new wife Margaret Elizabeth Lofty who he had met in Bath, but they were denied entry as he could not supply any references. Margaret thought his name was John Lloyd.

14 Bismarck Road (Waterlow Road), Highgate, N19 5NH

After being refused entry to 16 Orchard Road Margaret and George found rooms on Bismarck Road.

On December 18, 1914 Margaret Elizabeth Lofty was found dead in the bath on the first floor.

84 Islington High Street, N1 8EG

Margaret Elizabeth Lofty went to see solicitor Arthur Lewis, on December 18, to draw up a will leaving everything to her husband as sole executor of the will.

East Finchley Cemetery, 122 East End Road, N2 0RZ

On December 22, 1914 Margaret Elizabeth Lofty was buried here in an unmarked grave at the request of her husband.

14 Richmond Road, Shepherd's Bush, W12 8LY

George Smith went to find new rooms in Shepherd's Bush the day before the burial of his wife Margaret Elizabeth Lofty. He paid a deposit for a bedroom and returned on December 23, to say he would come back after Christmas.

60 Uxbridge Road, Shepherd's Bush, W12 8LP

Smith went to visit solicitor Arthur Davis, where he showed Margaret Lofty's birth certificate, marriage certificate, will and insurance policy. He was granted £705 minus fees.

Kentish Town Police Station, 10-12A Holmes Road, NW5 3AE

Following his arrest George Smith was taken to Kentish Town Police Station, where he took part in an identity parade where Charles Burnham (a relation of Alice Burnham) was able to identify him.

Bow Street Magistrates' Court, 4 Bow Street, WC2E 7AT

George Smith was charged with false entry into a marriage register when he married Margaret Lofty.

Following the later exhumations of his wives a number of hearings were held here.

Brixton Prison, Jebb Avenue, Brixton Hill, SW2 5XF

George Smith was held in Brixton prison as he awaited his trial.

Old Bailey, EC4M 7EH

Smith was committed for trial for the murder of Bessie Mundy on June 22, 1915. The jury took 22 minutes to decide he was guilty. He was sentenced to death and was sent to Maidstone prison on August 4, declaring his innocence all the way.

SERIAL KILLERS | 119

**60 Uxbridge Road,
Shepherd's Bush, W12 8LP**

Brixton Prison, Jebb Avenue, Brixton Hill, SW2 5XF. Courtesy of David Anstiss on Wikimedia Commons

During the trial, the jury were taken into a side room where there was a demonstration on how Smith committed the murder. The inspector carried out the technique on a nurse seated in a bath wearing a swimsuit. It worked so well the nurse needed to be resuscitated.

Smith was hanged on Friday, August 13, 1915 at 8am.

Soho Serial Killings (1935-1936)

A series of unsolved murders which took place in Soho in 1935/1936 are thought to be the work of a serial killer as all the victims were strangled in their own homes. However, not all were prostitutes and there seemed no obvious connection between them. No one was ever arrested for the crimes.

3-4 Archer Street, Piccadilly, W1D 7AP

Josephine Martin (known as French Fifi) had lived here since 1933. She was a Russian prostitute and was found by her maid on Monday, November 4, 1935 dead on her bed. She had been strangled with her own silk stockings.

47 Lexington Street, Soho, W1F 9AW

Marie Jeanet Cotton (née Cousins), a domestic servant lived in a

second floor flat on Lexington Street. She lived with an Italian chef, Carlo Lanza, and his 15-year-old son. She returned to the flat from work on Thursday April 16, 1935 at 1pm and spoke with a neighbour at 5pm.

At 9pm her body was discovered. She had been strangled with a silk stocking and the coroner thought death was about 6:30pm.

66 Old Compton Street, W1D 4UH

Leah Smith (also known as Hinds) was in a relationship with Stanley King who did conjuring tricks for a living. When he found out she was a prostitute he wanted her to give it up. By May 1936 they were living in a second floor flat here. She was found on May 9, 1936 by King when he finished his night shift.

She had been strangled with a thin wire and beaten with a flat iron. An unusual fingerprint had been found on the mantelpiece, so the police sliced off the corner of the wood and took it to the police station.

Prince Edward Theatre (was Palace Theatre), Old Compton Street, W1D 4HS

Just after midnight, Saturday May 9, 1936, Leah Smith left her friend Joan Maymar, as she needed to get some clients to make some money.

She was seen walking towards Wardour Street with a man before they were seen entering her flat at 12:30. It was the last time she was seen alive.

The Blackout Ripper (1942)

RAF cadet pilot Gordon Frederick Cummins was charged in 1942 with a series of murders which may have had both a sexual and financial element as the victims had all been robbed. He was identified through the number on his gas mask which he left at one of the scenes of attack.

He was charged with four murders and two attempted murders, although there are others who are thought to be victims despite remaining unsolved. The study of fingerprints found on a candlestick, bottle and tumbler in Mrs Lowe's room, and the tin opener and mirror in Evelyn Oatley's room were an important part of the investigation.

76 Gloucester Place, W1U 6DQ

Evelyn Hamilton was staying at lodging rooms at the Three Arts Club at 76 Gloucester Place at the time of her murder.

Maison Lyons Corner House, 1 Marble Arch, W1H 7DX

Evelyn Hamilton came here to eat dinner at about midnight on February 8, 1942 and had beetroot.

A national chain, the Maison Lyons were huge restaurants and department stores covering four to five levels with each floor featuring a different thematic restaurant and its own orchestra playing nonstop for patrons. They were all closed by 1977.

76 Gloucester Place, W1U 6DQ

Maison Lyons Corner House Teashop, 1 Marble Arch, W1H 7DX

At the time of writing the ground floor of this building had been completely remodelled, but the upper floors of the façade are as they would have looked in 1942.

Montagu Place (close to Gloucester Place), Marylebone, W1H 2ES
February 9, 1942 at about 8am the body of Evelyn Margaret Hamilton was found in a brick air-raid shelter on this street. She'd been strangled. There was no sign of struggle and no one saw anything.

Monico Restaurant, 39-45 Shaftesbury Avenue, W1D 6LA
Evelyn Oatley was seen outside this restaurant on Monday February 9, 1942 about 11pm, the night before her body was found in her first-floor bedsit on Wardour Street (the building has been demolished). Her body was found in her room on Tuesday February 10, 1942. She'd had her throat cut with a razor and her body mutilated with a tin opener. Fingerprints which helped identify Cummins as the murderer were found on the tin opener and mirror in her room.

The site is that of the Gielgud Theatre, which has units for restaurants.

Punch Bowl Pub, 41 Farm Street, W1J 5RP
www.butcombe.com/the-punchbowl-pub-mayfair

On Thursday February 12, Margaret Mary Heywood was attacked by the Blackout Ripper on this street outside the pub where he had kissed her and tried to pull her skirt up. When she resisted, he tried to strangle her, but he was disturbed by 18-year-old John Shine, who shone a torch on them. The Ripper ran away. This was about 9:45pm. He left behind his gas mask which bore his name and RAF number leading to his arrest.

29 Southwick Street, nr Sussex Gardens, Tyburnia, W2 1JQ
22-year-old prostitute Catherine Mulcahy aka Kathleen King lived here. She had taken Cummins back to her flat, where he kept boasting about how much money he had. She wasn't impressed as she wanted him to get on with it, so

29 Southwick Street, nr Sussex Gardens, Tyburnia, W2 1JQ

she could find another client. He was irritated by this and tried to strangle her. She managed to run from the flat in only her boots, to her neighbour Agnes Morris who rang the police.

9/10 Gosfield Street, W1W 6HD

Margaret Florence Campbell Lowe lived on Gosfield Street whilst she was working as a prostitute. She picked up clients on Charing Cross Road, Oxford Street and Piccadilly. She was known by the other girls as 'The Lady' or 'The Pearl' as she was well-spoken.

She was found in her flat on Friday February 13, 1942, after her friends and daughter hadn't seen her for two days. She had been strangled and her body mutilated after death.

Regent Palace Hotel, 36 Glasshouse Street, W1B 5AR

Margaret Lowe was last seen on Wednesday February 11 at half past midnight outside this hotel. She returned to her flat in Gosfield Street between 1:15-1:30am with a man who left at a later, unspecified time.

187 Sussex Gardens, Tyburnia, W2 2RH

The body of Doris Elizabeth Joaunnet was found in the ground floor flat of this building. She had been strangled and stabbed on the same day as Margaret Lowe (Friday February 13, 1942).

Doris had come to London from the North East of England and was working

9/10 Gosfield Street, W1W 6HD

as a prostitute. However, she did not need to live this lifestyle as she had a wealthy husband and an income.

Doris and her husband had had dinner together on the night of February 12, and they walked to Paddington station together as she saw him off to work. She then solicited on Sussex Gardens rather than heading home.

Royal Court Hotel, 7-12 Sloane Square, SW1W 8EG

Doris's husband, Alfred Joaunnet, was the manager at this hotel at the time

187 Sussex Gardens, Tyburnia, W2 2RH

of the murder. He stayed at the hotel whilst his wife stayed at the Sussex Gardens flat.

1 Gloucester Crescent, Regent's Park, NW1 7DS

Edith Humphries, 50, was stabbed in the head, strangled and found in her home on Gloucester Crescent on October 17, 1941.

She was a widow and worked as a cook at the Auxiliary Fire Station on Caledonian Road. The murderer was never caught but it is thought that Cummins could have been the killer.

Brixton Prison, Jebb Avenue, Brixton Hill, SW2 5XF

Gordon Frederick Cummins was held here after he was arrested. The evidence tied him to three of the murders: the tape on his watch matched some taken from Doris Joaunnet's home, his gas mask had traces of cement dust from the air-raid shelter where Evelyn Hamilton was found, a comb and pen matched dust outlines from Doris's home, a green propelling pencil identified as belonging to Evelyn Hamilton, and a piece of paper with Margaret Heywood's phone number on it. His shoes also matched footprints found in the snow.

Bow Street Magistrates' Court, 4 Bow Street, WC2E 7AT

On February 17 and March 26, 1942 Cummins appeared at the Bow Street Magistrates' Court. The public gallery was full, as they looked at him in his RAF greatcoat. He was to go to trial at the Old Bailey.

Old Bailey, EC4M 7EH

Cummins's trial started on April 23 where he was charged with four murders and two attempted murders. The evidence for Evelyn Oatley was the strongest. After a couple of false starts and two new juries, the trial took two days, and on April 28, 1942 the jury returned a guilty verdict.

47 Frith Street, W1D 4HT

Cummins claimed on the night of the murder of Evelyn Oatley he had been drinking with a colleague and had picked up two prostitutes, Molly Alven and Laura Denmark.

However, whilst he returned to the latter's flat on Frith Street he left at midnight, meaning this wasn't a strong enough alibi as he could have killed Oatley after midnight.

27 St James's Close, Regent's Park, NW8 7LQ

Throughout the period of the murders, Gordon Frederick Cummins was staying at the RAF barracks on this site and due to his posh-accent he was known as 'The Count,' 'The Duke' or 'The Honourable George Cummins.'

Wandsworth Prison, Heathfield Road, SW18 3HU

Cummins was executed on June 25, 1942 during an air raid. He professed his innocence to the end.

Acid Bath Murders (1945-9)

John Haigh had been a fraudster long before moving to London, spending time in prison for his crimes which included selling shares which didn't exist.

He confessed to the murder of Henrietta Durand-Deacon, Dr Archibald Henderson and Rosalie Henderson. He dissolved their bodies and non-valuable belongings in vats of acid in a workshop in Crawley. He murdered and disposed of the bodies of William McSwan, Donald McSwan and Amy McSwan in Gloucester Road.

He claimed to have drunk the blood of Durand-Deacon, the younger McSwan and the Hendersons. He was charged with murder on March 1, 1949 and sent to Lewes prison to await trail. He pleaded not guilty and his counsel tried to prove insanity to avoid the death penalty. The jury found him guilty and he was sentenced to death.

Onslow Court Hotel (The Kensington Hotel) 113 Queen's Gate, SW7 3LE

Suffragette Henrietta Olive Robarts Durand-Deacon and John Haigh were long-standing residents here in the 1940s. Durand-Deacon moved here in 1943. She disappeared on February 19, 1949 which was reported to the police the next day.

79 Gloucester Road, SW7 5BW

This was Haigh's flat where he claims to have dissolved the murdered bodies of William Donald McSwan, Amy McSwan and Donald McSwan in the basement flat of this building in 1945.

Haigh also claims to have killed a woman here and disposed of her body after meeting her in Hammersmith. This woman has never been identified and there is doubt that she actually existed. He moved out in July 1945.

Number 79 is currently a Comptoire Libanais (77a) and the

Onslow Court Hotel (The Kensington Hotel) 113 Queen's Gate, SW7 3LE

79 Gloucester Road, SW7 5BW

basement flat can no longer be seen from the street.

Goat Tavern, 3A Kensington High Street, W8 5NP

www.greeneking.co.uk/pubs/greater-london/goat-tavern

Haigh claimed to have met William Donald McSwan (the son) in this pub before heading back to 79 Gloucester Road. He had known the family since 1937, and he had agreed to 'help' the younger McSwan avoid conscription into the army - although perhaps not in the way Donald had in mind.

Donald was last seen on September 9, 1944. His parents were last seen on July 2, 1945.

Anglo Czech Welfare Association, 22 Ladbroke Square, W11 3NA

Haigh answered an advertisement by the Hendersons who were selling their property at 22 Ladbroke Square. He didn't purchase the property.

16 Dawes Road, Fulham, SW6 7EN

The Hendersons moved to this address from Ladbroke Square. It was here that Haigh acquired Dr Henderson's revolver which he used to murder him.

Haigh was able to acquire this property after the murders through forged deeds of transfers before selling it on. Through selling their assets he gained £7,771 (nearly £500,000 in today's money) which he lost through gambling.

9 Grand Drive, Raynes Park, SW20 0JB

This is one of four London properties owned by the McSwans which Haigh sold following their murders. In all he obtained nearly £5,500 which paid for his stay at the Onslow Court Hotel, a Lagonda sports car and his gambling habit.

Wandsworth Prison, Heathfield Road, SW18 3HU

Following the trial and sentencing Haigh was sent to Wandsworth prison. He was hanged on August 10, 1949 by Albert Pierrepoint.

There were 500 spectators to see the death notice pinned to the gate.

Ripper of Rillington Place (1953)

At 10 Rillington Place (Notting Hill) six female bodies were discovered, and all had been strangled. John Reginald Halliday Christie was charged and hanged for the murders.

There were two bodies in the wall; Kathleen Maloney, a prostitute who came to London in 1952 and was killed early January 1953, and Rita Elizabeth Nelson, also a prostitute who rented a room in Shepherd's Bush. She was killed on January 17, 1953 and was six months pregnant.

Hectorina Mackay Maclennan, wasn't a prostitute, and came to London with her family in 1948. She stayed with Christie along with Alexander Baker from March 3 to 5, 1953.

Ethel Christie née Simpson, John Christie's wife, was discovered under the floor.

Muriel Amelia Eady was last seen on October 7, 1944, and it was assumed she was killed in the bombings. Her body was found in the garden alongside Ruth Fuerst, an Austrian who arrived in Britain in 1939 as a refugee.

Beryl Evans and her 13-year-old daughter Geraldine lived and died at 10 Rillington Place. Her husband was charged and executed for their murders, but Christie later claimed he had also killed them although the details he gave were not accurate.

No 10 Rillington Place and the street were completely demolished in the 1970s and redeveloped.

6 Almeric Road, Battersea, SW11 1HL

John Christie lived here in 1929 with Maud Cole and her son. Following an argument when he was out of work he hit her with her son's cricket bat. He was sentenced to six months hard labour at Wandsworth prison.

Wandsworth Prison, Heathfield Road, SW18 3HU

Christie did a six-month stint hard labour for assaulting Maud Cole with the cricket bat in 1929.

23 Oxford Gardens, Notting Hill, W10 5UE

Following time in Wandsworth prison Christie was reunited with his wife, Ethel, and they lived here prior to moving to Rillington Place in 1927.

35 Oxford Gardens, Notting Hill, W10 5UF

Ruth Fuerst lived here in 1943, not far from Rillington Place. She was reported missing in August 1943 and was discovered in the garden of Rillington Place.

2-4 Lower Richmond Road, SW15 1JN

John Christie was arrested at the Welcome Café, Putney Bridge.

Today this is a restaurant called the Thai Square which sits on the footprint of the Welcome Café.

Notting Hill Police Station, 99-101 Ladbroke Road, W11 3PL

After his initial arrest, Christie was moved from Putney to Notting Hill Police Station where he was charged for the murder of his wife and questioned about the other bodies found at the house.

This was closed as a police station in 2021 and was empty at the time of writing.

Old Bailey, EC4M 7EH
John Christie went to trial at the Old Bailey for the murder of his wife on June 22, 1953.

The trial lasted only for four days. His defence led with a case of insanity.

Old Bailey, EC4M 7EH. Courtesy of GrindtXX on Wikimedia Commons

Brixton Prison, Jebb Avenue, Brixton Hill, SW2 5XF

Whilst awaiting trial Christie was held on remand in Brixton prison.

Pentonville Prison, Caledonian Road, N7 8TT

Christie was executed at Pentonville prison on July 15, 1953 by Albert Pierrepoint. A large crowd gathered to see the death notice on the gates.

Jack the Stripper (1963-5)

There were a series of murders in Hammersmith in the 1960s. The six victims were primarily prostitutes and their bodies were left near the Thames. Paint traces found at the scene of the murders were traced to a disused warehouse near a paint spray shop on the Heron Trading Estate. There were 20 workers at the site.

A security guard, Mungo Ireland, who worked nights committed suicide as he said he couldn't bear the strain anymore. Although never convicted, the killings stopped after his death although it has come to light that he was actually in Scotland when one of the murders took place.

The files on this case are in The National Archives and won't be released until 2050.

Duke's Meadow, Duke's Meadow Car Park, Chiswick, W4 2SH

The body of Elizabeth Figg was found on June 17, 1959 on Duke's Meadow and is thought to have been the first victim of Jack the Stripper. She had been a prostitute in Bayswater and had been strangled.

Barnes Borough Council Household Refuse Disposal Site, Townmead Road, TW9 4EL

The body of Welsh-born Gwyneth Rees was found on November 8, 1963 at the Barnes Borough Council household refuse disposal site on Townmead Road, Mortlake, 37 metres from the Thames towpath, and approximately 1.6 km from Duke's Meadows.

Rees was naked except for a single stocking on her right leg, extending no further up than the ankle. She had been accidentally decapitated by a shovel which workmen had been using to level the refuse.

27 Warriner Street, Battersea, SW11 4EA

Gwyneth Rees lived at this address until September 1963. She had been working as a prostitute at the time.

London Corinthian Sailing Club, (below Linden House), Hammersmith, W6 9TA

On Sunday February 2, 1964 George and Douglas Capon discovered Hannah Tailford's body under the pontoon here. Her body had been in the water for a couple of days before discovery. She had been strangled, and several of her teeth were missing.

37 Thurlby Road, West Norwood, SE27 0RN

Hannah Tailford (also been known as Anne Tailford, Teresa Bell and Anne Taylor) lived here with her two children, three-year-old Linda and 18-month-old Lawrence and her partner Alan Lynch. She had been charged on three accounts of prostitution, the last in 1963.

Corney Reach (access to underside of Barns Bridge via Thames Tradesmen's Rowing Club), Chiswick, W4 2SH

Irene Lockwood (aka Sandra Russell) was found dead on April 8, 1964 under Barnes Bridge, near Duke's Meadows, not far from where Tailford had been found. She had been in the river for approximately three days, and she was four months pregnant at the time of her murder.

It was only with the discovery of Lockwood that the police realised a serial killer was at large.

16 Denbigh Road, Notting Hill, W11 2SN

Irene Lockwood had lived at this address prior to being murdered. She paid £12 10s per week for rent.

Windmill Pub, 214 Chiswick High Road, W4 1SD

Archibald Kenneth, a caretaker at Holland Park lawn tennis club on Addison Road, Kensington, said he had met with Irene Lockwood here on April 7. After leaving the pub together, she asked him for money making

him lose his temper. He claimed he strangled her, stripped her and threw her in the river. He was arrested and charged with her murder.

This pub was demolished in 1964 to be replaced with an office block incorporating the pub at ground level.

Rebranded as Jack Stamp's Beer House in the 1990s, this closed in 2005. The pub is now in commercial use and is Megan's at the Flower Market restaurant.

Old Bailey, EC4M 7EH

Archibald Kenneth was taken to trial at the Old Bailey but it was thrown out and he was said to be a fantasist who made up his involvement due to depression. He then admitted to never having met Irene Lockwood.

199 Boston Manor Road, off Swyncombe Avenue, Brentford, TW8 9LE

Scottish-born Helen Barthelemy (who was also known as Helen Paul, Teddie Thompson and Teddie Paul) was found dead here on April 24, 1964.

Near her body were flecks of paint which was commonly used in car manufacturing and was the first potential link to the killer.

34 Talbot Road, W2 5LJ

Helen Barthelemy lived in the ground floor flat on this road. She was a prostitute and striptease artist. The last clear sighting was at 10pm on Monday April 20, 1964, by Ivy Williams who saw she had a visitor in her flat - although whether male of female was unknown. She had popped out to get fish and chips for her guest.

48 Berrymede Road, Chiswick, W4 5JD
Scottish-born Mary Theresa Fleming (aka Mary Theresa Turner) was found dead on July 14, 1964 on the drive of this house.

Her false teeth were missing, but again paint spots were also found on the body. Many neighbours had also heard a car reversing down the street just before the body was discovered. She was unlikely to have been killed here, but instead dumped here by the killer.

44 Lancaster Road, Notting Hill, W11 1QR
Mary Fleming lived in a ground floor one bedroom flat here. She had been convicted for prostitution and had two children, two-year-old Veronica and nine-month-old David. She was reported missing when there was no one to look after the children on July 11, 1964.

Kensington Central Library, Kensington, W8 7RX
Another Scot, Frances Brown (aka Margaret McGowen, Frances Quin and Alice Sutherland), was a prostitute and was last seen alive on October 23, 1964 by a colleague who saw her get into a client's car. The car was identified as a grey Ford Zephyr.

On November 25, her body was found in a car park on Hornton Street, which is now where Kensington Library is located. She had been strangled.

16a Southerton Road, Hammersmith, W6 0PH
This was the last known address of Frances Brown. She was a prostitute who worked around the Notting Hill and Bayswater areas.

The Castle Pub (was Warwick Castle Pub), 225 Portobello Road, W11 1LU
www.castleportobello.co.uk

On October 23, 1964 Kim/Kay Taylor spent the day with Frances Brown which included going for a drink here. Mary Fleming, a previous victim, also drank in this pub.

When they left the pub, they got into two cars with Kim/Kay's car intending on following the first (a dark grey Zephyr or Zodiac) with Frances and her client inside.

They were planning to meet at The Jazz Club, Notting Hill but the car was lost on the Bayswater Road and Frances wasn't seen alive again.

Heron Trading Estate, 14 Alliance Court, Alliance Road, W3 0RB
Irish immigrant Bridget "Bridie" O'Hara was found dead on February 16, 1965 near a storage shed behind the Heron Trading Estate.

She had been missing since January 11. Once again, there were flecks of industrial paint on the body which were traced to an electrical transformer near where she was discovered.

This was also the site where the potential murder suspect worked as a security guard.

Sindercombe Social (was Shepherd's Bush Hotel), 2 Goldhawk Road, W12 8QD

This was the last place that Bridie O'Hara was seen, leaving the bar at closing time on January 11, 1965. She was seen leaving in a car.

Sindercobe Social Club (was Shepherd's Bush Hotel), 2 Goldhawk Road, W12 8QD

MISCELLANEOUS CRIMES

Vandalism

Islington Local History Centre, Patrick Coman House, 245 Skinner Street, EC1V 4NE

Visits by appointment only
local.history@islington.gov.uk

In 1962 Joe Orton and Kenneth Halliwell were placed on trial for the theft and 'malicious damage' of books belonging to Islington Public Library. Orton claimed their actions were a protest against the poor choice of books available in public libraries at the time.

The 'malicious damage' was to 'doctor' the covers and blurbs of the books with collage, and a tongue in cheek commentary on the contents.

They were both found guilty and sentenced to six months' imprisonment for their elaborate literary prank. 41 of these book covers are preserved and on display here.

Poverty

13 Red Lion Square, WC1R 4QH

In the 1820s it was illegal to be poor to a certain extent. In 1824 the Vagrancy Act was passed which meant it was illegal to beg, and therefore beggars could be arrested for vagrancy. At a time with no social services many of London's poor had to beg in order to stay alive. In 1821 a bill was presented (but failed) to remove all poor relief from able bodied people.

The offices of London Society of the Suppression of Mendicity stood at 13 Red Lion Square. They sent out plainclothes officers to arrest people for vagrancy and bring them back here before handing them over to the authorities.

In 1831 the 'Dicity' reported on the 671 people they had detained: 64 (mostly women) were destitute through death, desertion or imprisonment of a husband or loved one. Four were foreign and couldn't afford the fare home, one lost everything in a fire, another in a shipwreck, 61 had been injured or were ill, six had no decent clothes to find work, and another seven had no tools to carry out their trade.

Those arrested for vagrancy could be imprisoned and sentenced to hard labour.

Forty Elephants

The 40 Elephants Cocktail Bar, 3-5 Great Scotland Yard, SW1A 2HN

www.hyattrestaurants.com/en/dining/uk/london/internationalrestaurant-in-westminster-the-40-elephants

This bar is named after and dedicated to the infamous group of smash and grab shoplifting women called the Forty Elephants, who were active between the 1920s and 1950s. The cocktails are named after aspects of the gang's activity (for example, the 'On the Run,' or 'Forger' in honour of Shirley Pitts), and there is a small display of artefacts connected to the gang.

They are open for food and drink seven days a week.

The Globe Tavern, 8 Bedale Street, SE1 9AL

Alice Diamond, the leader of the Forty Elephants, came from a criminal background. Her father Thomas Diamond (Junior) was arrested with

The 40 Elephants Cocktail Bar, 3-5 Great Scotland Yard, SW1A 2HN

The Globe Tavern, 8 Bedale Street, SE1 9AL

eight other men for attacking PC John Fogwell outside this pub in 1888.

St George's Hall, 5 Westminster Bridge Road, SE1 7XW
During an election meeting at St George's Hall on October 1, 1900 a disturbance broke out when questions about housing were not answered by the mayor and other councillors. People were ejected from the building and the doors shut.

Thomas Diamond was seen punching the Lord Mayor's son, Harry Kottingham Newton so hard his head was propelled through a window. Kottingham Newton had been locked out of the building by mistake. Diamond was imprisoned for two months for this offence.

This building has been currently standing empty for a number of years.

Criminal Sculptor (1886)

Statue of Queen Anne, St Paul's Churchyard, EC4M 8AD
The statue of Queen Anne is a nineteenth century copy of a 1712

Statue of Queen Anne, St Paul's Churchyard, EC4M 8AD

sculpture by Francis Bird on the same location. The original was in a sorry state, so it was decided to commission a copy to be made. The original is at the Ridge in Hastings.

Richard Claude Belt was commissioned to do the work in 1885. Like many artists he led an unconventional life, and shortly after accepting the commission he was arrested and imprisoned for 12 months for fraud in early 1886.

In the press it was reported that he was given permission to complete the statue whilst in Holloway prison.

Instead the sculptor, Louis-Auguste Malempré was brought in to finish the sculpture and he demanded a retraction in the press, as did Queen Victoria herself.

When Belt was released from prison he demanded his name was put on the statue.

The Siege of Muswell Hill (1965)

65 Woodland Rise, Muswell Hill, N10 3UN

On June 6, 1965 three policemen knocked on this door looking for Eileen Blackman, who had escaped from Holloway prison. As they knocked two bullets were fired through the door at them.

What followed was a 90-minute siege where Eileen fired her .22 Winchester from a first-floor window at anyone who came close. She hit one constable.

She was eventually arrested and another five years were added onto her sentence.

RELATED SITES

EXECUTION SITES

Whilst there were major execution sites across London, public executions could actually be held in any public place, or close to where the crime was committed as a form of deterrent.

Executions had for centuries been a public spectacle, an opportunity to head out with friends and family, eat well and buy souvenirs with the hope that there would be a good 'last speech' or an attempted rescue. Samuel Pepys in 1660 went to the execution of Major General Harrison, who was hanged, drawn and quartered, as well as the execution of Colonel John Turner in 1664, for which he paid a shilling to stand on the wheel of a cart to get a better view.

By the mid-1800s this form of entertainment was no longer considered civilised and the ethics of execution were debated. Dickens comments that the execution of Francois Courvoisier in 1840 was "nothing but ribaldry, debauchery, levity, drunkenness and flaunting vice" and later described executions as a "moral evil".

In 1864 the Royal Commission for Capital Punishment was set up and it was two years before public executions were prohibited putting them behind closed doors. The Irish Republican Michael Barrett was the last person to be publicly executed on May 26, 1868. However, it was to be nearly a century before executions in England were banned in 1969 and 1973 in Northern Ireland. However, it was still possible to be executed for Treason until the Crime and Disorder Act 1998 when it was finally abolished.

Town of Ramsgate Pub (was Execution Dock), 62 Wapping High Street, E1W 2PL
www.townoframsgate.pub

From 1360-1834 piracy, murder, mutiny and treason carried out at sea were tried by the High Court of Admiralty and those found guilty were executed at Execution Dock in Wapping. Gallows were set up in the foreshore at low tide and the bodies were left there until three tides had washed over them.

The final hangings on Execution Dock were on December 16, 1830 of George

Davis and William Watts, who were charged with piracy.

Although the exact location for the site is disputed, the Town of Ramsgate pub is thought to be the closest. The pub has been on the site since 1545, so it could have been a place to grab a drink before or after the executions even if the site wasn't visible from the pub itself.

Smithfield, Grand Avenue, EC1A 9PS
In 1305 Scottish nobleman William Wallace was executed here for treason. By the Tudor period Smithfield was an important execution site and equalled Newgate and Tyburn in regard to numbers. Throughout the sixteenth century it was also a common site for the burning of heretics who then became known as the Smithfield Martyrs. Henry VIII had Sir Thomas More, John Fisher and the Bishop of Rochester executed here. Some people who were burned to death here took more than two hours to die.

The last person burned at the stake for being a religious dissenter was Bartholomew Legate in 1612.

The market which currently sits on the site was designed by Sir Horace Jones in the later nineteenth century.

St Giles-in-the-Fields Churchyard, St Giles High Street, WC2H 8LG
The churchyard here in the nineteenth century was accused of "revolting ill-treatment of the dead."

Coffins were visible through the surface soil, and often they were

St Giles-in-the-Fields Churchyard, St Giles High Street, WC2H 8LG

broken up and removed to the charnel house before they had been in the ground for a fair amount of time.

The cemetery also contains the bodies of many of the people who went to the gallows at Newgate which was very close to the site.

St Bartholomew's Hospital, West Smithfield, EC1A 7BE
In 1555 St Bartholomew's was used for the burning of heretics during the reign of Queen Mary. She was notorious

for executing Protestants even if they recanted their religion.

In the centre of the square in front of the hospital, less than a metre down is a thick layer of ash which is said to be the remains of these executions. There is a blue plaque here for William Wallace and the Smithfield Martyrs.

Newgate Prison (now Old Bailey), EC1A 7AA

Between 1690 and 1780 criminals who committed crimes inside or near Newgate were executed outside the prison. In 1783 they erected a 'new drop' (trapdoor) gallows and it became the main site of executions. The Murder Act of 1752 stated those sentenced to death were to be executed two days after the sentencing, three days if they were sentenced on a Saturday meaning there was little time to appeal.

In the nineteenth century, houses opposite the prison were rented out to sightseers in order to have a good view of the public executions. They were charged between 20-50 guineas for the day. In 1846 there was a mass hanging of seven pirates and there were as many as 2,000 people attending.

After the public hangings, the ropes were often sold as souvenirs in pubs on Fleet Street.

The body of one man, William Duel, aged 16, who was hanged for rape and murder was sold to the doctors for study. Although showing no signs of

Tower of London, EC3N 4AB

life on the journey he revived upon the surgeon's table. He was returned to Newgate Prison where he was later transported to the USA.

By 1868 at least 1,130 men and women were executed here.

Tower of London, EC3N 4AB
www.hrp.org.uk/tower-of-london

The Tower of London was a notorious prison for hundreds of years and included gallows in the grounds for the execution of nobility and royalty.

Within the Tower of London is Tower Green which is next to the Chapel of St Peter ad Vincula. The executions which took place here were not public in the same way as the other execution sites but they were still not private affairs and were attended by the nobility.

In 1536 Anne Boleyn, Henry VIII's second wife, was executed here on fabricated charges of adultery as she was unable to produce a male heir, as well as his fifth wife Catherine Howard in 1541, also for adultery.

In 1541 Henry had Margaret Pole, Countess of Salisbury executed here for treason. She was 67 years old and unlikely to pose a threat to the king. However, she refused to lie down on the block claiming, "so should traitors, and I am none!" She was chased around the scaffold avoiding the axe-man's blows until she was eventually hacked to death. There is a memorial sculpture by artist, Brian Catling, on the site dedicated to all the people executed here.

Tower Hill, EC3N 4DX
Between 1388 and 1780, 120 people were executed publicly on Tower Hill. The site was founded by Edward IV (1442-1470) as permanent gallows on what was a rubbish tip.

Often these executions were beheadings including high profile traitors such as the leaders of the Jacobite rebellion in 1746, political figures like Thomas Wentworth in 1641 or Thomas More (1535) who disagreed with Henry VIII's reformation of the church and Thomas Cromwell (1540) who had brokered Henry's disastrous marriage to Anne of Cleves. Essentially anyone who went against the king on any grounds.

Now the site has been turned into the Trinity Square Gardens, which is

Trinity Square Gardens, Tower Hill, EC3N 4DX

dominated by the memorial for the WWI soldiers.

The Temple Bar Memorial, EC4A 2LT
The Temple Bar was used to display the heads of traitors of the state, although this was moved to Hertfordshire in 1878 after 200 years on the site.

Following the bar's removal, the Temple Bar Memorial was put in its place. The monument depicting a griffin, stands in centre of the road.

In 1684 a group of roundhead soldiers attempted to murder the king, Charles II, and his brother James II, in what became known as the Rye House Plot. The lead conspirator Sir Thomas Armstrong was executed and his body carved up and boiled in salt to prevent it being eaten by birds.

His co-conspirators' heads were impaled on spikes at the Temple Bar. Telescopes were hired out to visitors so they were able to see

the faces up close. One head was said to have remained in place for thirty years.

Tyburn (Marble Arch), W1C 1LX

The junction between Edgware Road and Oxford Street marks Tyburn, which between 1196 and 1783 was used as a place of execution. At the time, it was open country and was on the main route to Oxford, which is why Tyburn Road was renamed as Oxford Street.

The earliest execution here was William FitzOzbert or 'Longbeard' on April 6, 1196. He was hanged, drawn and quartered for treason, as he planned to overthrow the king.

He had been dragged behind a horse for the five miles from the Tower of London before he was hanged at Tyburn. FitzOzbert was not only the first to be executed at Tyburn, but also the first to become a martyr.

Executions took place from the Triple Tree or Tyburn Tree, a triangular gallows which could hang multiple people from 1571. There were also gibbets here where the bodies were displayed as a deterrent.

Condemned prisoners were often brought from Newgate on the back of a cart. When they reached Tyburn, the hangman put a noose around their neck, and as the cart drove away they were left hanging, dying of strangulation.

In the nineteenth century stands were erected where people could pay a fee for the best view. Mother Proctor had a pew from 1724 and earned £500 (£50K in modern money) at the execution of Earl Ferrers in 1760. It is thought that as many as 50,000 people may have been executed at Tyburn throughout the years of usage.

Many of the bodies of the executed prisoners were buried in pits at the site, and when digging the pedestrian walkways at Marble Arch in 1961 hundreds of human remains were found including one body still with iron shackles around their ankles.

Lincoln's Inn Fields, WC2A 3BP

In the sixteenth century Lincoln's Inn Fields was also an execution ground, and in 1586, Anthony Babington and his co-conspirators were hanged, drawn and quartered here for attempting to overthrow Elizabeth I and replace her with Mary, Queen of Scots.

Lincoln's Inn Fields, WC2A 3BP

This execution was considered one of the most brutal to take place on the site.

The Additional Ground in Drury Lane (Now Drury Lane Gardens), 57 Drury Lane, WC2B 5SN

This churchyard, like every other in London was overcrowded, and burials were often a lot closer to the surface than six feet.

This churchyard contained the burial of Richard Brandon, who executed Charles I in 1649 outside the Banqueting House in Whitehall. The execution was unpopular and thousands of people gathered for Brandon's funeral yelling things like "Bury him in the dunghill!"

The building to the right of the gate is all that remains of the church, which was bombed in the Second World War, and was the mortuary which held the dead bodies before burial.

Hounslow Heath, Hanworth Road, Hounslow, TW4 5LJ

In the 1770s as many as 100 gibbets were set up on Hounslow Heath following the 1752 Murder Act which allowed the

The Additional Ground in Drury Lane (Now Drury Lane Gardens), 57 Drury Lane, WC2B 5SN

Kennington Common, Kennington Park Road, SE11 4PP

corpses of murderers to be displayed as a deterrent.

Poet Robert Southey stated: "from whatever quarter the wind blew it brought with it a cadaverous and pestilential odour."

Think of this as you take a walk through the Heath.

Kennington Common, Kennington Park Road, SE11 4PP

The Surrey Gallows was located here (100 metres from Oval Underground). Between 1678 and 1800, this was the primary execution site for the county of Surrey.

The common was bigger than it is now, and the church is now on the site of the gallows. There is a plaque giving the history of the area within the church grounds.

Newington Green (was Horsemonger Lane Gaol), Harper Road, SE1 6PP

In 1800 the Surrey County Gaol was built on Horsemonger Lane in Southwark and executions were transferred from Kennington Common to the roof of the gatehouse where the new drop method could execute seven criminals at a time.

The executions were therefore very public. The most famous execution here was in 1849 of husband and wife Frederik and Maria Manning, for murdering Patrick O'Connor, Maria's Lover. They were hanged together.

The first executions here were on Friday April 4, 1800, when five men were hanged for coining, highway robbery, being at large and two for burglary. 126 were hanged there publicly and five more in private between 1868 and 1877.

The gaol was demolished in 1881 and was replaced by Newington Gardens.

PRISONS

East

Viaduct Tavern, 126 Newgate Street, EC1 7AA
www.viaducttavern.co.uk

Many sources state the cellars of the Viaduct Tavern were once part of Newgate Prison. However, this simply isn't true, and we have included this pub to dispel the myth.

The Viaduct Tavern was built in 1869 and was always well outside the walls of Newgate Prison. There was, however, some crossover in dates between the prison and the pub, as Newgate wasn't demolished until 1904, but they were never connected.

Other sources state the Viaduct Tavern was built on the site of the Giltspur Street Compter debtor's prison, and the original cells are in the cellar. This also isn't true. The Museum of London recorded in 1998: "The [Giltspur Street Compter] prison was closed in 1853 and demolished in 1854, this work entailed the extensive robbing out of the below ground foundations."

So, the Viaduct Tavern doesn't have cells in the basement, or feeding tubes on the street outside (they are coal holes), but it does have gin, and boasts it is a 'Traditional Gin Palace,' and therefore is worth visiting for that alone as well as for the beautiful Victorian décor.

Tower of London, EC3N 4AB
www.hrp.org.uk/tower-of-london

The Tower of London was built as a fortress with the earliest building being the White Tower in 1070, and over the years has had many uses including that of prison. The earliest recorded prisoner was Bishop Ranulf Flambard in 1110, who was chief tax collector under William Rufus (William II) and was imprisoned for extortion. He was allowed servants and used his wealth to pay for food and wine. In February 1120, he threw a feast for the prison staff, and when they were drunk he escaped using a rope which had been smuggled in via a vat of wine. He was therefore the first man to escape the Tower as well.

In March 1554, the princess Elizabeth Tudor (later Elizabeth I) arrived at Traitor's Gate at the behest of Queen Mary. Her mother Anne Boleyn had been at the Tower 19 years earlier and had been beheaded in Tower Green. Elizabeth no doubt thought this was also to be her fate, but four years later she was released at the death of Queen Mary and crowned queen. Many of the prisoners incarcerated here carved their name onto the walls of their cells.

At the foot of the White Tower in 1674, workmen discovered a wooden chest with the skeletons of two children. In 1933 they were forensically examined and said to be the remains of two princes Edward (aged 12) and Richard (aged 9) who were held in the Tower in 1483 for their own protection whilst there were various coups regarding the throne of England. Richard III claimed they were the bastard sons of Edward IV, and they promptly disappeared. To this day no one knows who murdered them.

Reggie and Ronnie Kray were two of the last people to be held prisoner in the Tower of London in 1952. They spent a few days here after going AWOL from the army and before they were shipped to Shepton Mallet military prison to await court martial.

Old Bailey (was Newgate Prison), EC4M 7EH

Newgate was notorious with a reputation for being one of London's most corrupt prisons. Daniel Defoe (1703) was once incarcerated here and described it in his novel 'Moll Flanders';

> "The hellish noise, the roaring swelling and clamour, the stench and nastiness ... an emblem of hell itself."

The wealthier you were the easier a stay here was as prisoners paid for room and board, but conditions were so bad that prisoners were bathed in vinegar before their court appearances to disguise their unpleasant odour.

It was situated on the corner of Newgate Street and Old Bailey Street and shares a footprint with the Old Bailey which was built on the site in 1904. Many of the bricks from Newgate were incorporated into the new building.

There was a courtroom attached to Newgate Prison, known as the Old Bailey and was used for crimes within the City of London and Middlesex. In the nineteenth century this was extended to include all major trials throughout England. Then as now trials were open to the public, but in the eighteenth and nineteenth centuries visitors were charged a penny to enter.

Until 1920 juries were all male and in the eighteenth and nineteenth centuries if it was thought they were taking too long to come to a decision they were refused food, drink and heat.

North

Holloway Prison, Parkhurst Road, N7 0NU

Holloway prison was opened in 1852, and was originally a mixed-sex prison, although by 1903 it was changed to a women's prison.

It was closed in 2015, with the intention of selling the site for residential development.

Pentonville Prison, Caledonian Road, N7 8TT

Pentonville is a category B men's prison and was opened in 1816 to house 860 prisoners. It was used in the twentieth century as a site of execution following the closure of Newgate in 1904. 161 men were executed here between 1902 and 1967.

As it is a working prison please be cautious of security if trying to take photographs.

South

Belmarsh Prison, Western Way, SE28 0EB

Belmarsh is a category A male prison, which was opened in 1991, and is still in operation today. It houses various categories of prisoners but prisoners primarily are from Old Bailey trials.

As it is a working prison please be cautious of security if trying to take photographs.

Brixton Prison, Jebb Avenue, Brixton Hill, SW2 5XF

Brixton prison was built in 1821 and was originally called the Surrey House of Correction. Early prisoners here were sentenced to work on a treadmill in order to mill corn. It originally housed both men and women.

In 2012 the prison was downgraded to a category C training facility where prisoners are able to take educational courses and vocational training.

As it is a working prison please be cautious of security if trying to take photographs.

Wandsworth Prison, Heathfield Road, SW18 3HU

Wandsworth prison was built in 1851 as the Surrey House of Correction and was built as part of the separate system principle where corridors radiate from a central point. It is one of the largest prisons in the UK.

It was also an execution site and between 1878 and 1961 there were as many as 135 executions here.

POLICE STATIONS

North

Kentish Town Police Station, 10-12A Holmes Road, NW5 3AE

In 1933 Samuel Furnace was arrested in Southend and brought to Kentish Town Police Station where he claimed the shooting of Walter Spatchett had been accidental when he was 'showing' Walter the revolver. He claims he 'lost' his head and decided to burn the body.

The Brides in the Bath killer, George Smith, was also brought here in 1914 following his arrest.

Willesden Police Station, 96 High Road, NW10 2PP

Ruby Spark, the smash and grab raider, was taken to Willesden Police Station, where he produced false identity before eventually admitting he was Charles Ruby Spark.

The police station was built in 1896 and is currently empty but plans have been presented for a large residential redevelopment.

South

4 Whitehall Place, SW1A 2EG

4 Whitehall Place was the site of the original police headquarters in 1829 when the Metropolitan Police Act was passed by Parliament.

It backs onto Great Scotland Yard therefore giving it the name which is used to this day. By 1887, Scotland

4 Whitehall Place, SW1A 2EG

Yard had expanded into 3, 5, 21 and 22 Whitehall Place as well as 8 and 9 Great Scotland Yard.

They were relocated in 1890 to larger premises on Victoria Embankment.

Norman Shaw Buildings, Victoria Embankment, SW1A 2JH

In 1890 the Metropolitan Police Headquarters relocated from Whitehall Place to Victoria Embankment to what is now called the Norman Shaw Buildings. Since 1829 the force had grown from 1,000 officers to 13,000 and needed more space. The buildings were designed by Richard Norman Shaw and John Dixon Butler.

The police moved again in 1967, and since 1979 the Norman Shaw Buildings have been parliamentary buildings.

New Scotland Yard, Victoria Embankment, SW1A 2JL

The Metropolitan Police Headquarters have been at this site since 1967 and can be seen in the background of numerous news reports and police interviews.

Norman Shaw Buildings, Victoria Embankment, SW1A 2JH

New Scotland Yard, Victoria Embankment, SW1A 2JL

West

Chiswick Police Station, 209-211 Chiswick High Road, W4 2DU

Micky McAvoy was interviewed at Chiswick Police Station where he refused to give any answers regarding his involvement in the Brink's-Mat Robbery.

Notting Hill Police Station, 99-101 Ladbroke Road, W11 3PL

John Christie was brought to Notting Hill Police Station following his arrest where he was charged with the murder of his wife and questioned about the other bodies found at the house at 10 Rillington Place.

Shepherd's Bush Police Station, 252 Uxbridge Road, W12 7JA

On August 12, 1966, the three police officers PC Roger Fox, PC Wombwell and PS Head, murdered in the Braybook Street Massacre all started their shift at Shepherd's Bush Police Station.

At the time of writing the police station has been permanently closed and was standing derelict.

Coram's Fields, 93 Guilford Street, WC1N 1DN

On September 26, 1829, after the Metropolitan Police Act was passed by Parliament the new recruits of the Metropolitan Police went on their first parade in the grounds of what was the Foundling Hospital in Holborn.

The site is now a children's playground run by a charity. Nearby is the Foundling Museum, which will tell you more about the history of the site.

Bow Street Police Station, 4 Bow Street, WC2E 7AT

After his arrest, Dr Thomas Neill Cream was brought here in 1891 and charged with murder as was Udham Singh (aka Singh Azad) in 1940 following his assassination attempts and actual murder at Caxton Hall and Edwin Bush following the murder at Cecil Court in 1961.

This was the site of the Bow Street Magistrates' Court as well and the home of the Bow Street Runners and later the Metropolitan Police. The first court was opened in 1740 and closed in 2006.

Smallest Police Station, Trafalgar Square, WC2N 5DN

The world record holder for being Britain's Smallest Police Station can be found in Trafalgar Square.

The base of one of the square's lamppost plinths was hollowed out in 1927, enabling accommodation for one police officer who could then keep watch over Trafalgar Square which has always been a gathering place for protests and troublemakers.

There was a phone within the box which connected to police HQ and should the police officer use the phone the light on top of the station flashed, alerting any officers nearby that there was a disturbance in the square. The light is often stated to be one from Nelson's HMS *Victory*, but this is not true and instead is a 'Bude Light' which was designed by Sir Goldsworthy Gurney.

Today the police station is no longer used by the police and is instead used for storage by Westminster Council.

West Drayton Police Station, Station Road, West Drayton, Uxbridge, UB7 7JQ

Brian Robinson was taken to West Drayton Police Station where he provided what appeared to be a solid alibi regarding his involvement in the Brink's-Mat Robbery.

Smallest Police Station, Trafalgar Square, WC2N 5DN

MUSEUMS

East

Jack the Ripper Museum, 12 Cable Street, E1 8JJ
www.jacktherippermuseum.com

This is a small museum laid out over five floors of a Victorian house and offers an insight into the lives of the women of the East End in the 1880s, as well as the identities of some of the suspects at the time.

The Gunpowder Plot Immersive Experience, 8-12 Tower Hill Vaults, EC3N 4EE
www.gunpowderimmersive.com

This exhibition is an immersive experience with live actors taking you through the intrigue and mistrust around the time of the Gunpowder Plot.

West

Bow Street Police Museum, 28 Bow Street, WC2E 7AW
www.bowstreetpolicemuseum.org.uk

The site of the Bow Street Magistrates' Court was the home of the Bow Street Runners and later the Metropolitan Police. The first court was opened in 1740 and closed in 2006.

This is now a Grade II listed building and is the home of the Police Museum where cells have been made into galleries to tell the story of policing in the area.

London Dungeon, Riverside Building, County Hall, Westminster Bridge Road, London SE1 7PB
www.thedungeons.com/london/whats-inside/what-is-the-dungeon/jack-the-ripper

The London Dungeon is a museum experience which takes you back to the darker past of London and includes an exhibit of the Guy Fawkes Gunpowder Plot, and a visit with the fictional Sweeney Todd.

At the time of writing there is currently a Jack the Ripper exhibition here. Here you will be led through a tour by the landlady of the Ten Bells pub as she talks you through the murders.

Jack the Ripper Museum, 12 Cable Street, E1 8JJ

SPECIALIST TOURS

Tyburn Procession

In the eighteenth century once a prisoner had been condemned to death they made the 4.5km procession to Tyburn from Newgate Prison for hanging.

The procession took place eight times a year and the prisoners were transported in an open cart, sitting on the coffins which would later be used for their bodies. The route was lined with crowds meaning this journey could take as long as three hours.

The route took them down Holborn, St Giles High Street, and up Tyburn Road (Oxford Street) with stops and rituals being held along the way. Not all of the stops are still standing, but the main route is still walkable with plenty of old buildings along the way.

Newgate Prison, Old Bailey, EC4M 7EH

Newgate Prison stood on the corner of Newgate Street and Old Bailey Street. It had been built in 1188 and pulled down in 1902. The Old Bailey was then built on the footprint of Newgate, and even used some of the masonry in its construction.

For most of its history it was a prison, but by the end of the eighteenth century executions were moved from Tyburn to Newgate. These were very public and many of the surrounding houses rented out rooms so people could get unhindered views from the windows.

Holy Sepulchre Church, Holborn Viaduct, EC1A 2DQ

One of the first stops from Newgate, was at the Holy Sepulchre Church. Here the bellman rang a hand bell which the condemned had last heard at Newgate at midnight. The bells here were only rung on a day there was to be a hanging.

There was a recital of prayers and then the condemned was given a small bunch of flowers on the steps of the church. It was a noisy rather than a sombre affair, and on November 16, 1724 more than 100,000 people followed the procession of the thief, Jack Sheppard.

Masons Arms, (now The Portman) 51 Upper Berkeley Street, W1H 7QW
www.theportmanw1.com

It was common for the procession to stop for refreshments in the form of

158 | THE TRUE CRIME LOVER'S GUIDE TO LONDON

Masons Arms, (now The Portman) 51 Upper Berkeley Street, W1H 7QW

gin, at the Masons Arms on Seymour Place. This is now The Portman, a gastro pub but it is possible to have a quick gin in memoriam.

St Giles High Street, WC2H 8AB

The procession also stopped at St Giles-in-the-fields, which is now St Giles High Street, at some of the inns there for a quick tipple. This was potentially a mercy stop as it enabled many of the prisoners to get drunk to the point of unconsciousness before they reached Tyburn.

Whilst the road has been redeveloped and none of the bars along this road are original, the church, St Giles-in-the-fields was one of the buildings the condemned passed.

Tyburn (Marble Arch), W2 2UH

As you continue walking along St Giles High Street, it changes to Denmark Street. At the end you turn right onto Charing Cross Road, and then left onto Oxford Street, following the route to Tyburn at Marble Arch. This was originally called Tyburn Road, but as it was the main route to Oxford it was changed to Oxford Street.

Tyburn was on the junction between Edgware Road and Oxford Street and was in use as an execution site from 1196 to 1783.

From 1571, executions took place from the Triple Tree or Tyburn Tree, which was a triangular gallows which could hang multiple people at once.

St Giles High Street, WC2H 8AB

There were also gibbets here where the bodies were on display as a deterrent.

In the eighteenth-century stands were erected where people paid a fee for the best view. Mother Proctor had a pew from 1724 and earned £500 (£50K in modern money) at the execution of Earl Ferrers in 1760.

It is thought that as many as 50,000 people may have been executed at Tyburn throughout the years.

CHURCH TOUR

East

St George-in-the-East Church, 14 Cannon Street Road, E1 0BH
The memorial for the seven victims of the Ratcliff Highway Murders was held in the parish church of St George-in-the-East. The baby had been baptised there only three months before the murders.

Holy Sepulchre Church, Holborn Viaduct, EC1A 2DQ
One of the first stops from Newgate to Tyburn for the condemned criminals, was at the Holy Sepulchre Church. Here the bellman rang a hand bell which the condemned had last heard at Newgate at midnight. The bells here were only rung on execution days.

There was a recital of prayers and the condemned was given a small bunch of flowers on the steps of the church. It was a noisy rather than a sombre affair, and on November 16, 1724 more than 100,000 people followed the procession of the thief, Jack Sheppard.

St Mary-le-Bow Church, St Mary-le-Bow Church, Cheapside, EC2V 6AU
William FitzOzbert or 'Longbeard' in 1196 was known for challenging authority, and during a siege following his public denouncement of the throne he killed a Kingsman. In his panic he fled and sought sanctuary in this church and hid here with nine of his conspirators.

The King's Men went against protocol and started a fire in the grounds of the church in order to 'smoke' the conspirators out so they could be arrested.

West

Parish Church of St Stephen and St Thomas, 1 Coverdale Road, W12 8JJ
On August 31, 1966, the three policemen killed on Braybrook Street in Shepherd's Bush were buried following a ceremony in St Mary-le-Bow church. There were 600 policemen on the route of the funeral procession.

St Paul's Church (Watch House), Bedford Street, WC2E 9ED
The body of the murdered Italian Boy, Carlo Ferrier, was taken to St Paul's Watch House on November 6, 1831 to be examined and to determine the cause of death.

The watch house stood to the left of the entrance gateway, approached by the steps and filled the gap between the gateway and NatWest.

St Giles-in-the-Fields Churchyard, St Giles High Street, WC2H 8LG
The churchyard here in the nineteenth century was accused of disrespectful treatment of the dead and coffins were

visible through the surface soil and were often broken up and removed to the charnel house before they had been in the ground for long.

The cemetery also contains the bodies of many executed criminals from Newgate.

South

St George the Martyr, Borough High Street, SE1 1JA
www.stgeorge-themartyr.co.uk

In 1777, a body snatcher attempted to steal a corpse from the graveyard at St George the Martyr and was caught. This was the first prosecution for body snatching to take place, although it was a crime which was well-known at the time.

St Nicholas' Church, Deptford Green, SE8 3DQ
Amelia Goodman married Joseph Winters, on January 29, 1854 here. They went on to have at least five children.

Amelia Winters is the only known female serial killer in London.

St Margaret's Church, St Margaret Street, SW1P 3JX
www.westminster-abbey.org/st-margarets-church

In 1863, the doors from St Margaret's Church Westminster leading to the treasury were thought to be covered in the skin of William the Sacrist who was responsible for the Westminster Abbey theft in 1303.

Today the Abbey claim the skin is cowhide. Even so, the door is Britain's oldest and leads to the Chapter House.

St Mary's Church, Saint Marychurch Street, SE16 4NF
The body of Jack 'The Hat' McVitie was dumped outside this church, although it was quickly moved before the police got to it.

The Kray twins and their gang were soon arrested for the murder.

Outskirts

St Mary's Church, Church Street, Old Amersham, HP7 0DB
www.stmaryschurchamersham.com

Ruth Ellis, the last women hanged was originally buried in an unmarked grave in Holloway prison, but in the 1970s she was exhumed and reburied in the graveyard of St Mary's Church.

Although technically in Buckinghamshire, this churchyard is a 15-minute walk from Amersham underground station.

CEMETERY TOUR

It's hard to imagine what nineteenth century London burial grounds were like. They were overcrowded, unkempt, and rather than being the restful landscaped places they often are today, the ground surface could be scattered with coffin wood, and nails and body parts were often protruding through the ground.

Burial grounds were a money maker and in addition to state-run or church-run cemeteries, there were private yards where a premium was paid for interment. That didn't, however, mean the dead were treated with any more respect, and these were often more crowded than the public cemeteries. One private cemetery, which was raised in Parliament in 1842, had more than 2,300 bodies per acre per year.

Graveyard owners commonly dug up recent burials as a means of making way for further burials in order to increase their income. Often this was taken too far, as people were being dug up, and their coffins dismantled for sale when they had only been in the ground for a few weeks. The bones were wheeled away in a cart to be dumped in a 'bone house' (ossuary or charnel) in order to make room for more bodies.

Bodies were frequently buried on top of bodies until they were only a few inches from the surface, with limbs sometimes protruding through the surface. St Martin's, Drury Lane was recorded as having so many bodies that the level of the graveyard had actually reached the first-floor windows of the surrounding buildings. They were smelly, distressing places and due to the sheer volume of bodies cemeteries also contaminated drinking water.

In 1832 a bill was passed which allowed for seven new cemeteries to be built on the outskirts of London in order to alleviate the pressure on the smaller graveyards within the city. These were:

- 1840 - Abney Park Cemetery, N16 0LH
- 1840 - Brompton Cemetery, SW10 9UG
- 1839 - Highgate Cemetery, Swains Lane, N6 6PJ
- 1833 - Kensal Green Cemetery, Harrow Road, W10 4RA
- 1840 - Nunhead Cemetery, Linden Grove, SE15 3LP
- 1841 - Tower Hamlets Cemetery, Southern Grove, E3 4PX
- 1837 - West Norwood Cemetery, Norwood Road, SE27 9JU

Some of these cemeteries were also connected with crime in one way or another.

North

East Finchley Cemetery, 122 East End Road, N2 0RZ

On December 22, 1914 Margaret Elizabeth Lofty was buried in an unmarked grave, following her murder by Brides in the Bath killer, George Joseph Smith.

Edmonton Cemetery, Church Street, N9 9HP

Hatton Garden robber Danny Jones told the police when he was in prison that he had buried his share of the loot in the cemetery. He said he buried it in two graves of male relatives of his wife, Val Hart, but would only reveal which ones when he was released.

The police were able to recover some of the stolen jewellery from the memorial stone of his father-in-law, Sidney James Hart. They didn't tell Danny of their discovery, and when they took him to the cemetery on October 15, 2015 he led them to the grave of Sidney John Hart, where a smaller stash was uncovered. He was adamant this was all the jewellery there was.

East

Sheen's Burial Ground, 52-58 Commercial Road and 109-153 Back Church Lane, E1 1LP

On July 23, 1825, a man was thrown into a grave at this private burial ground in an attempt to bury him alive.

The day before, his wife Lucer had died in hospital following a beating. He refused to have her buried according to Irish and Catholic tradition which saw her funeral at Sheen's Burial Ground. As her body was lowered into the grave, the 8-10,000 strong crowd attempted to throw him in as well.

The burial ground has been turned into green space in front of large-scale blocks of flats between Gower's Walk and Back Church Lane.

Alderney Road Cemetery, Stepney, E1 4EG

This cemetery was very aware it could be the victim of the dreaded resurrection men, who exhumed bodies to sell to surgeons and medical schools.

When burials were carried out here, a wheeled sentry-box was used and moved around the cemetery so people could keep an eye on new burials for a number of nights after the burial had taken place.

Globe Fields Whitechapel (Now Globe Road Memorial Gardens), E2 0LE

In October 1839 police were called to this burial ground after a witness working for the Eastern Counties Railway Company, saw two men and a boy, digging up the bodies in one part of the burial ground and throwing them into a large pit they had dug on the other side.

The police pulled over a young lad with a bag of nails and human bones which he claimed he was going to sell. It was common to chop up coffins to sell the wood and nails, but also to make room for more burials in the churchyards which brought an income into the church.

It is currently a memorial garden, next to the Victory Life Baptist Church.

Chingford Mount Cemetery, 121 Old Church Road, E4 6ST

Ronnie Kray died in March 1995 in prison, and Reggie Kray was allowed parole early as he was suffering from inoperable cancer in 2000. He died within a month on October 1, 2000.

They are buried alongside their brother Charlie Kray who also died in 2000, their mother Violet and father Charlie, Reggie's wife Frances and Charlie Jnr's son Gary.

To find the graves, from the entrance walk down North Way towards the top left-hand corner of the cemetery. They are placed on the corner of Memorial Way and Remembrance Walk.

Manor Park Cemetery, Sebert Road, Forest Gate, E7 0NP

Mary Ann Chapman was the second victim of Jack the Ripper and is buried in Manor Park Cemetery. There is a small plaque marking the grave.

Once you walk through the entrance, walk along the grass path between two trees on your left. Continue walking until the graves get a little older. The plaque is on the left.

City of London Cemetery, Aldersbrook Road, E12 5DQ

Mary Ann Nichols, the first Jack the Ripper victim was buried at City of London Cemetery, in an unmarked grave although there is now a plaque commemorating her death.

To find her plaque head towards the red-roofed traditional crematorium, walk anti-clockwise around it and walk along the path until you pass the pond on your right. Turn left on Memorial Way and keep walking until you find the marker.

The commemorative plaque to the fourth victim, Catherine Eddowes can be found a little further along the path. She was also buried in an unmarked pauper's grave.

Chingford Mount Cemetery, 121 Old Church Road, E4 6ST

East London Cemetery, Grange Road, E13 0HB

Two of Jack the Ripper's victims are buried in East London Cemetery; Elizabeth Stride and Frances Coles as well as possible victim Alice McKenzie, who was nicknamed Clay Pipe Alice.

Elizabeth was buried in a pauper's grave, which has since been upgraded with a marble surround. To find the grave, walk towards the war memorial, and turn left along the path. Follow the main path to the right, and then bear left along a gravel path.

Frances Coles was known as Carroty Nell because of her red hair. She was buried close to Elizabeth Stride although we were unable to locate a marker for her or Alice Mckenzie.

Walthamstow (St Patrick's) Roman Catholic Cemetery, Queen's Road, E17 8QP

Mary Jane Kelly the fifth victim of Jack the Ripper was buried in St Patrick's Roman Catholic Cemetery.

Her obituary announced that "no family member could be found to attend the funeral" but due to the horrific nature of her death her funeral had hundreds of attendees.

East London Cemetery, Grange Road, E13 0HB

Walthamstow (St Patrick's) Roman Catholic Cemetery.

The exact location of her burial isn't known, but there is a marker in what is thought to be the approximate spot. When you walk through the gates of the cemetery, keep to the left of the chapel building, walk past the large McCarthy family grave, and turn left on the path. As you walk down the path you will see a statue of a footballer, and Mary's marker is just behind that.

Mary Spink who was murdered by her husband George Chapman, was also buried here on December 30, 1897, in a common grave without a headstone.

Her body was exhumed for post-mortem on December 9, 1902.

South

Crossbones Cemetery, Union Street, SE1 1SD

www.crossbones.org.uk

Between the sixteenth century and 1853, this unconsecrated burial ground was used "for the interment of the low women who frequented the neighbourhood," and for the paupers and those who were forbidden from being buried in a churchyard.

It was closed as a burial ground in 1853 due to the overcrowding and the land sold in 1883 as a building site.

In the 1920s during building work, forty bodies were uncovered and reburied in Brockwood Cemetery in Woking. In the 1990s and the extension of the Jubilee Line, 148 further bodies were uncovered.

Crossbones Cemetery, Union Street, SE1 1SD

In 2014 it was set up as a memorial garden.

Brockley Cemetery, 113 Brockley Grove, SE4 1DZ
Elizabeth Jane Frost, Sidney Bolton and William Sutton, victims of the Deptford Poisoner Amelia Winters were buried here.

Amelia Winters was also buried here on July 22, 1889 in unconsecrated ground. The (unmarked) grave was under two lime trees, between the cemetery wall and a footpath, near the graves of Bolton, Sutton and Frost.

Tooting Cemetery, Blackshaw Road, Tooting, SW17 0BY
Matilda Clover, a victim of Thomas Cream, was buried here on October 22, 1891.

West

The Additional Ground in Drury Lane (now Drury Lane Gardens), 57 Drury Lane, WC2B 5SN
This churchyard contained the burial of Richard Brandon, who executed Charles I in 1649. The execution was unpopular and thousands of people gathered for Brandon's funeral yelling things like "Bury him in the dunghill!"

The building to the right of the gate is all that remains of the church, which had been bombed in the Second World War, and was the mortuary which held the dead bodies before burial.

PUB CRAWL

The pub was an important element of London social life for decades, as the place where people met to socialise, to talk business, to meet the opposite sex, to look for murder victims and to plan and commit crimes. Here is a tour of all the pubs discussed in this book, enabling you to visit some of the most notorious taverns in London history. We don't recommend doing the tour on one day, but if you do, drink responsibly.

North

Castle Pub, 54 Pentonville Road, N1 9HF
www.thecastleislington.co.uk

Danny Jones, Terry Perkins and Kenny Collins met here regularly from as early as 2012 to plan the Hatton Garden Heist.

The pub is open seven days a week for food and drink and they broadcast major sporting events.

Ye Olde Cherry Tree Pub, The Green, N14 6EN
www.vintageinn.co.uk/restaurants/london/yeoldecherrytreesouthgate

On April 24, 2015 Danny Jones, Terry Perkins and Kenny Collins met up here to discuss selling the loot stolen from Hatton Garden and how to make the handovers.

The pub is open seven days a week for food and drink and is dog friendly.

The Rocket (was The Rising Sun), 120 Euston Road, NW1 2AL
www.therocketeustonroad.co.uk

Emily Dimmock, a prostitute in 1907 met some of her clients in this pub, including Robert Wood, an artist who worked for the London Sand Blast Decorative Glass Works on Grays Inn Road. Wood was eventually charged with her murder but was acquitted and the murder has never been solved.

This pub is open seven days a week and is available for food or drinks.

Old Eagle Pub, 251 Royal College Street, NW1 9LU
On the night of Emily Dimmock's murder, September 11, 1907 she spent time in this pub before heading to her home on Agar Grove. The killer entered her home and slit her throat whilst she slept.

This pub is open seven days a week and is available for food or drinks.

Magdala Public House, South Hill Park, NW3 2SB
www.themagdala.co.uk

On Easter Sunday 1955, Ruth Ellis followed her boyfriend David Blakely to the Magdala where she waited for him to emerge. As he walked towards his car, she pulled the gun out. He glanced at her and then ignored her. She shot him at point blank range, and then when he was on the floor emptied the chamber into him.

They are open seven days a week for food and drink.

East

Ten Bells Pub, 84 Commercial Street, E1 6QQ
www.tenbells.com

On the night of November 8, 1888, prostitute Mary Kelly, stopped off at the Ten Bells pub, where she often picked up clients. She was the last of Jack the Ripper's victims.

In the 1930s the landlady, Annie Chapman renamed the pub Jack the Ripper, but it has since returned to the original name and retains a number of original features.

They are open seven days a week for food and drink, and they call themselves an 'historic east end boozer.'

Culpeper Pub (was Princess Alice), 40 Commercial Street, E1 6TB
www.theculpeper.com

Frances Coles came to the Princess Alice on February 11, 1891 and met up with James Sadler, an old client of hers. They spent three days and two nights together, and he bought her a new hat. She was found dead on February 13 and was thought to be a Jack the Ripper victim.

The top floor has recently been added and there is a roof garden. They are open for food and drink.

Blind Beggar Pub, 337 Whitechapel Road, E1 1BU
www.theblindbeggar.com

George Cornell was murdered here by Ronnie Kray in 1966. Ronnie entered the pub with John Barrie and shot Cornell through the eye. No one 'saw' anything as they were too afraid of the Krays.

This pub is open for drinks and food seven days a week and has a garden for the summer.

The Carpenters Arms, 73 Cheshire Street, Bethnal Green, E2 6EG
This pub was bought by the Krays in 1967 for their mother Violet. They used it for

Blind Beggar Pub, 337 Whitechapel Road, E1 1BU. internal

various business meetings over the years, and on October 29, 1967 Reggie had a drink here before killing Jack McVitie.

They open seven days a week and have a basic food menu.

The Gun Tavern, Docklands, 27 Coldharbour, E14 9NS

www.thegundocklands.com

This early eighteenth-century pub was used by Lord Nelson to meet Emma Hamilton in what is now the River Room.

There is also an enclosed staircase which has a smugglers' spy hole cut into the wall and was used by smugglers evading the revenue officers.

This pub offers food and drink, as well as showing major sporting events. It is open seven days a week but closes at 10pm on Monday and Tuesday.

Viaduct Tavern, 126 Newgate Street, EC1 7AA

www.viaducttavern.co.uk

Many sources state the cellars of this pub were once part of Newgate Prison, but this isn't true.

The Viaduct Tavern was built in 1869 and was always well outside the walls of Newgate Prison which stood on the exact footprint of the Old Bailey opposite. Newgate was demolished in 1904.

Other sources state the Viaduct Tavern was built on the site of the Giltspur Street Compter debtor's prison, and the original cells are in the cellar. This also isn't true.

So, the Viaduct Tavern doesn't have cells in the basement, or feeding tubes on the street outside (they are coal holes), but it does have gin, and boasts it is a 'Traditional Gin Palace,' and is worth visiting for the beautiful Victorian décor and the food.

It is closed on Sundays.

The Castle Farringdon, 34-35 Cowcross Street, EC1M 6DB

www.thecastlefarringdon.co.uk

On May 1, 2015 Terry Perkins and Kenny Collins met Brian Reader here. It was the first meeting with Brian since the Hatton Garden robbery and was tense. It was here that the police recorded the meeting and employed a lip reader to interpret what they were saying.

They are open seven days a week for food and drink.

Town of Ramsgate Pub (was Execution Dock), 62 Wapping High Street, London E1W 2PL

www.townoframsgate.pub

From 1360-1834 piracy, murder, mutiny and treason carried out at sea were tried by the High Court of Admiralty and those found guilty were executed at Execution Dock in Wapping. Gallows were set up in the foreshore at low tide and the bodies were left there until three tides had washed over them. This was practiced until the early nineteenth century.

The Castle Farringdon, 34-35 Cowcross Street, EC1M 6DB

Although the exact location for the site is disputed the Town of Ramsgate Pub is thought to be the closest.

This pub has been on the site since 1545, is open seven days a week and serves food and drink.

The Fox, 28 Paul Street, Shoreditch, EC2A 4LB

www.thefoxpublichouse.co.uk

Following the Security Express Robbery in 1983, John Horsley hid the sacks of money in his garage and also built a false back into a cupboard at his father-in-law's flat where he hid a further £270,000 for Billy Hickson.

A false wall was also discovered by police at John Knight's pub, The Fox, where some of the cash had been stored. The pub had once been managed by Clifford Saxe who was also involved in the robbery.

The hole smelt of mildew and old beer which matched the smell on some of the recovered money.

When John was arrested his brother Ronnie, who was once married to Barbara Windsor, fled to Spain.

South

The Brockley Barge (was The Breakspeare Arms), 184 Brockley Road, SE4 2RR

www.jdwetherspoon.com/pub-histories/england/london/the-brockley-barge-brockley

This pub was the site of some of the inquests in the Deptford poisonings. On April 18 1889, the inquest of Sidney Bolton was started here, and then on June 1 following the exhumation of William Sutton it continued until July 9.

Until the 1990s the pub was called the Breakspeare Arms. It was then closed due to getting a bad reputation for violence and drugs. Now it is a Wetherspoons and has been rebranded as the Brockley Barge.

This pub is open seven days a week and serves good value food and drink.

The 40 Elephants Cocktail Bar, 3-5 Great Scotland Yard, SW1A 2HN

www.hyattrestaurants.com/en/dining/uk/london/international-restaurant-in-westminster-the-40-elephants

This bar is named after the infamous group of smash and grab shoplifting women called the Forty Elephants (aka Forty Thieves), who were active between the 1920s and 1950s. The cocktails are named after aspects of the gang's activity, and there is a small display of artefacts connected to the gang.

They are open for food and drink seven days a week.

Plumbers Arms, 14 Lower Belgrave Street, SW1W 0LN

www.greeneking.co.uk/pubs/greater-london/plumbers-arms

Following the night of the murder of Sandra Rivett, Veronica Mary Duncan fled the house and headed to the Plumbers Arms to raise the alarm.

At the inquest into Rivett's death, held in June 1975, the jury returned a verdict naming Lord Lucan as her killer.

This pub serves food and drink but is closed on Sundays.

Nag's Head, 53 Kinnerton Street, Knightsbridge, SW1X 8ED

Margery Gardner who was found dead in her bed in 1946, was a regular here. She was working as a film extra as she waited for her art career to take off.

Neville Heath, who was dishonourably discharged from the RAF and was calling himself Lieutenant Colonel Bill Armstrong of the South African Army was also a regular here. He was seen drinking with Margery on June 20, the night before her murder.

The Nag's Head is open seven days a week for food and drink.

West

The Portman (was Masons Arms), 51 Upper Berkeley Street, W1H 7QW
www.theportmanw1.com

The Masons Arms was a regular stop-off before the nineteenth century on the procession leading from Newgate Prison to the execution site at Tyburn.

The condemned and the warders (and no doubt many of the followers) grabbed a glass of gin here to fortify them for the task ahead.

It is now The Portman, a gastro pub which is open seven days a week, with early closure on a Sunday.

Punch Bowl Pub, St Alban's Street, 41 Farm Street, W1J 5RP
www.butcombe.com/the-punchbowl-pub-mayfair

On Thursday February 12, 1942 Margaret Mary Heywood was attacked by the Blackout Ripper on this street, outside the pub where he kissed her and tried to pull her skirt up. When she resisted, he

Punch Bowl Pub, 41 Farm Street, W1J 5RP

tried to strangle her, but was disturbed by 18-year-old John Shine, who shone a torch on them. The Blackout Ripper ran away. This was about 9:45pm. He left behind his gas mask which bore his name and RAF number leading to Gordon Frederick Cummins' arrest.

Northumberland Arms Pub, 119 Tottenham Court Road, W1T 5AW
www.greatukpubs.co.uk/northumberland-arms-bloomsbury

On October 21, 1891, Louisa Harris aka Loo Harvey met Dr Thomas Neill Cream who claimed to be a doctor from St Thomas's. He promised to cure her of some spots on her forehead. They met at this pub where he gave her some pills and then arranged to meet her later. She didn't take the pills, which was a lucky escape for her.

This pub is open seven days a week and serves food and drink.

35 Dorset Street, W1U 6QR
www.barleymowlondon.co.uk

Jack the Ripper victim Annie Chapman was staying at a lodging house at number 35 Dorset Street. which was run by Timothy Donovan. She arrived on midnight of September 7, 1888, drunk. She told Tim to hold the bed for her as she was short of the rent and therefore went out again at about 1:50am.

The building houses the Barley Mow pub which was established in 1791. Food is served Monday to Saturday.

Goat Tavern, 3A Kensington High Street, W8 5NP

Goat Tavern, 3A Kensington High Street, W8 5NP
www.greeneking.co.uk/pubs/greater-london/goat-tavern

John Haigh, the Acid Bath Murderer, claimed to have met one of his victims, William Donald McSwan (the son) in this pub. He offered to 'help' McSwan avoid conscription into the army. He was last seen alive on September 9, 1944.

This pub serves food and drink and is open seven days a week.

The Castle (was Warwick Castle Pub), 225 Portobello Road, W11 1LU
www.castleportobello.co.uk

On October 23, 1964 Kay/Kim Taylor spent the day with Frances Brown which included going for a drink here. This was the last day that Frances Brown was seen alive as she fell victim to the Jack the Stripper serial killer.

This pub offers food and drink as well as showing major sporting events. It is opposite the 'blue door' from the movie *Notting Hill*.

Sindercombe Social (was Shepherd's Bush Hotel), 2 Goldhawk Road, W12 8QD
www.thesindercombesocial.co.uk

This was the last place that Bridie O'Hara was seen, leaving the bar at closing time on January 11, 1965. She was seen leaving in a car and was one of Jack the Stripper's victims.

They are open seven days a week and serve food and drink.

MURDER LOCATIONS TOUR

North

97 Evering Road, Stoke Newington, N16 7SJ

On October 29, 1967 Jack 'The Hat' McVitie, was invited to a party in Blonde Carol's flat in Stoke Newington, being promised a 'party, birds and booze.' The party was in the basement flat of 97 Evering Road. The Krays got there first and removed all the other guests.

When McVitie arrived, Reggie Kray attempted to shoot him, but the gun jammed and instead stabbed him in the face, chest and stomach numerous times.

14 Bismarck Road (Waterlow Road), Highgate, N19 5NH

After being refused a room at 16 Orchard Road Margaret Elizabeth Lofty and George Smith found rooms here at 14 Bismarck Road.

On December 18, 1914 Margaret Elizabeth Lofty was found dead in the bath on the first floor.

1 Gloucester Crescent, Regent's Park, NW1 7DS

Edith Humphries, 50, was stabbed in the head, strangled and found in her home on Gloucester Crescent on October 17, 1941.

She was a widow and worked as a cook at the Auxiliary Fire Station on Caledonian Road. The murderer was never caught but it is thought that it was likely to be Gordon Frederick Cummins.

30 Hawley Crescent, NW1 8QR

On the evening on January 3, 1933, Mr Wynne, noticed that his shed in his back garden was on fire. When the fire brigade extinguished it, they discovered a burnt body inside.

The body was identified by a tenant as being that of Samuel Furnace. However, at the coroner's court, the judge examined the body and discovered a bullet wound in his back and the teeth were of a much younger man than Sam Furnace. Further examination of the body uncovered a post office book identifying him as 25-year-old Walter Spatchett who had been shot before being set on fire.

Sam Furnace who lived at Crogsland Road, left a note at his address which read; "Goodbye all. No work, no money, Sam J Furnace.' Crogsland street has been heavily refurbished.

The Hawley Crescent building is now Poppies fish and chip restaurant and has been heavily re-constructed.

29 Agar Grove (was St Paul's Road), NW1 9UG

Emily Dimmock (aka Phyllis) was murdered on September 11, 1907. She was working as a prostitute, although her husband, Bertram Shaw wasn't aware of her profession. She worked when he was on night shifts.

Emily Dimmock and her husband lived here, and this was where her body was found.

Magdala Public House, South Hill Park, NW3 2SB

www.themagdala.co.uk

On Sunday, April 10, 1955 Ruth Ellis followed David Blakely to the Magdala where she waited for him to emerge. As he walked towards his car, she pulled the gun out. He glanced at her and then ignored her. She shot him at point blank range, and then when he was on the floor emptied the chamber into him.

East

29 Hanbury Street, Spitalfields, E1 6QR

On Saturday September 8, 1888, Annie Chapman (née Smith, aged 47) was discovered near the steps to the doorway of the back yard of 29 Hanbury Street. She had been thrown out of a doss house at 2am and had nowhere to go, so was walking the streets when she came across Jack the Ripper. Her possessions had been lain at her feet including two brass rings, a few pennies and two farthings.

The buildings on the opposite side of the road give an idea of what it would have looked like, but number 29 is a modern building.

Henriques Street (was Dutfield's Yard, off Berner Street), E1 1NT

Jack the Ripper's third victim, Elizabeth Stride was discovered in Dutfield's Yard or Berner Street which is now Henriques Street on Sunday, September 30, 1888.

Born near Gothenburg in Sweden, Elizabeth was 44 when she died. She had some flowers pinned to her dress as she looked for customers.

Elizabeth Stride was seen outside 58 Berner Street with a man talking at 11:45pm on the night she died.

Jack had been disturbed whilst killing her and went on to kill another the same night.

Dutfield's Yard was between 40 and 42 Berner Street. The buildings on either side of the road were cleared for the Harry Gosling Primary school.

Blind Beggar Pub, 337 Whitechapel Road, E1 1BU

www.theblindbeggar.com

This was the location of the murder of George Cornell on March 10, 1966.

He was a member of a south London gang and had taunted Ronnie Kray about his homosexuality in the past.

Cornell had come north of the river and was drinking in the Blind Beggar. Ronnie was in another pub when he heard Cornell was here.

He entered the Blind Beggar with John Barrie and shot Cornell through the eye.

215 Whitechapel Road, E1 1DE

Opposite Henry Wainwright's shop was the warehouse for his brush-making business. Henry killed Harriet Louisa Lane, in 1874 at his shop, burying her beneath the floor of the paint room, covered in quicklime. Local workmen had heard gunshots between 5pm and 6pm, but thought it was a local eccentric who was known to have shot a gun at times. A post-mortem on the remains showed she had been shot in the head and then had her throat slit.

A year later, on September 11, 1875 Henry with his brother, Thomas Wainwright, removed the body and dismembered it to make disposal easier.

When he was moving from his shop he asked a friend Alfred Phillip Stokes to help him. He also told him he had a hammer, shovel and chopper which he would give Stokes to sell on.

Stokes became suspicious of the two badly smelling parcels and when Wainwright went to get a cab, he looked inside one and saw a human head. Wainwright returned with the cab, and Stokes was too scared to confront him so he followed the cab and called a policeman.

Today Henry's shop is Mahir (London) clothes shop.

31 Turner Street, E1 2AS

John Goodman Levy, a Jewish fence, was murdered at this address on April 4, 1896. In the morning of April 4, the housekeeper Annie Gale was seen opening the shutters and talking to the dairyman.

At 1pm, Miss Laughton arrived for lunch following an invitation from Mr Levy but received no answer when she knocked. She called on a neighbour, William Schafer to see what was happening. He went around the back and saw a man bent over in the outhouse, who fled into the basement when he realised he had been seen.

Mr Levy was found murdered in the outhouse, and the housekeeper, Mrs Gale was found dead in the top floor front bedroom. They had both been hit with a hammer, before having their throats cut.

When the police arrived, there was a disturbance when it was realised the murderer, William Seaman had made his way through a hole in the ceiling and the attic and was on the roof. He stepped onto the parapet and fell 40 feet to the ground. A small girl broke his fall.

The top floor of the building as it currently stands is a modern addition.

Pinchin Street, E1 1SA

A female torso was found under a railway arch in Pinchin Street in the early hours of the morning of September 11, 1889. As the site was close to Berner Street where Elizabeth Stride was discovered some thought it could also have been the work of Jack the Ripper, although the *modus operandi* was different.

45 Chamber Street, E1 8BL

In 1891, the railway arches on Chamber Street were open allowing passage through to the other side.

The body of Frances Coles was found under the last arch on this road at 2:15am on February 13. She was still alive when the police found her, which prevented them from following the footsteps they could hear running away from the site. Her throat had been cut twice and she died shortly afterwards.

James Sadler, her partner was arrested for the murder but was released on March 3 for lack of evidence. Some believe she was a victim of Jack the Ripper.

Old Castle Street (was Castle Alley), Whitechapel, E6 1PP

Alice McKenzie was discovered in Castle Alley on July 17, 1889 and is thought by some to be a Ripper victim although this killer appeared to be left-handed, whereas Jack the Ripper was right-handed.

She left her digs in Gun Street and was last seen alive at 11:40pm in Brick Lane.

Her throat had been cut and there were stab wounds on her abdomen. She was murdered between 12:30 and 12:45am. Her body was found just past the Wash Houses on the same side of the street, under a streetlamp.

This building is particularly interesting as it is just the façade of the original wash house with a completely new building behind.

126 Long Acre, EC2E 9PE

On September 5, 1948 Helen Freedman/Freeman a Lithuanian prostitute was found stabbed to death in her flat on Long Acre.

She was known as Russian Dora and had clearly fought for her life. Her flat was in a state of disarray, and there was a carving knife near her body bearing a fingerprint.

She was 56 but was able to make herself look much younger when she went out and had convinced a 26-year-old Canadian to propose although he changed his mind when he found out her age.

No one was ever arrested for the murder.

Mitre Square, EC3A 5DE

Jack the Ripper's fourth victim was Catherine Eddowes, who was discovered Sunday September 30, 1888, lying in Mitre Square. She had spent the evening in a police cell at Bishopsgate Police Station and had been released at 12:30am. It wasn't long until her body was discovered.

Her body was taken to The City of London Mortuary and Coroner's Court, Golden Lane, EC1Y 0QT. The original building was damaged in the Second World War.

Temple, EC4Y 9DA

On February 15, 1733 Sarah Malcolm murdered three people at the Temple.

She was a charwoman at the Inns of Court and strangled her employer, Lydia

Duncome, her companion, Mrs Harrison and silenced a maidservant Ann, by slitting her throat. When a neighbour, Mrs Love arrived for an appointment and received no answer she persuaded a laundress to climb through the fourth-floor window, where she discovered the bodies.

Sarah also stole £300 of jewellery, cash and plate.

South

Caxton Hall, 8-10 Caxton Street, SW1H 0AQ

On March 13, 1940 there was a meeting at Caxton Hall of the east India Association and the Royal Central Asian Society. There were 160 people there to hear the lecture, 'Afghanistan the Present Position.'

When the meeting was wrapping up, Udham Singh (aka Singh Azad) walked down the aisle and shot six bullets onto the stage from his .45 Smith and Wesson revolver. The bullets however were .44 and were thirty years old. He was also carrying a knife.

Sir Michael O'Dwyer was shot twice in the back, Sir Louis Dane's arm was broken by a bullet, Lord Lamington injured his wrist and Lord Zetland, although hit twice survived.

86 Rochester Row, SW1P 1LJ

John Robinson, an estate agent worked in a second-floor office at this address. He hailed a taxi from outside the office

86 Rochester Row, SW1P 1LJ

and got the driver to help him carry a heavy trunk from the office. He then went to Charing Cross Station.

His building was directly opposite the old police station on Rochester Row and has since been rebuilt.

45 Chester Square, SW1W 9EA

In the 1940s this house was rented by King George II of Greece who had been exiled during the war. He employed a housekeeper, Elizabeth McLindon, who had been a former prostitute. She was engaged to Arthur Boyce who had been instrumental in forging her references for the position. He was already married and had been in prison for bigamy and was wanted for cheque fraud.

On June 9, 1946, the king came to the property and was rather put out that there was no one there to greet him and the house hadn't been prepared. When the police broke into the servants' quarters they found Elizabeth dead, seated at the table, with a bullet wound to the back of the head.

46 Lower Belgrave Street, SW1W 0LN

On Thursday, November 7, 1974 Sandra Rivett was murdered at this address. The house belonged to Richard John Bingham, 7th Earl of Lucan, more commonly known as Lord Lucan and his wife Veronica Mary Duncan.

On the night of the murder Sandra, the nanny, was not meant to be working, and had planned to spend the night at her boyfriend's house. She put the children to bed at about 8:55pm and then offered to make Veronica a cup of tea. She headed to the basement kitchen where an assailant was waiting and bludgeoned her to death.

Veronica came down the stairs to see what had happened to the tea when Sandra did not return and was also hit over the head. Veronica later identified the assailant as her husband and while he washed himself in the family bathroom, she made her escape.

79 Gloucester Road, SW7 5BW

This was John Haigh's flat where he claims to have dissolved the murdered bodies of William Donald McSwan, Amy McSwan and Donald McSwan in the basement flat of this building in 1945. Haigh also claims to have killed a woman here and disposed of her body after meeting her in Hammersmith. This woman has never been identified and there is doubt that she actually existed. He moved out in July 1945.

Number 79 is currently a Comptoire Libanais (77a) and the basement flat can no longer be seen from the street.

13a Finborough Road, SW10 9DF

Prostitute Olive Young (real name Gertrude Yates) lived in the basement flat at number 13, 1922. Ronald True stayed overnight at her flat and stole £5 from her when he left. She swore she wouldn't see him again but he kept visiting and calling her.

On March 2, 3 and 4, 1922 he had driven to her house but she was out. However, she was in on March 5 and he spent the night with her.

On March 6, about 7:30 in the morning, he made them both a cup of tea and as she sat up in bed to drink it he beat her to death. She was only 25.

He told the daily, Emily Steel when she arrived at 9:15 not to disturb Olive as she was still sleeping. True stayed at the house until about 9:50. Olive's body was discovered at about 10:15.

13a Finborough Road, SW10 9DF

35 Lindesfarne Road, Wimbledon, SW20 0NW

Percy Arthur Casserley and his wife Georgina May (Ena) Casserley lived here in the late 1930s. They were married in 1927.

In the spring of 1937, the house next door to the Casserley's was being built and Mrs Casserley started an affair with the young foreman, Edward Royal Chaplin.

In September 1937, Ena Casserley discovered she was pregnant. Her husband was in a nursing home for alcoholism and she wrote to him for a divorce. He refused.

He returned home on March 22, 1938. He was murdered the next day.

She had arranged to meet Edward, and they went to nearby Copse Hill. She told him she was afraid to go home, so he said, "you had better leave this to me," and returned home with her. She heard a scuffle between her lover and her husband and then two gunshots. Chaplin emerged unscathed.

27 Lambeth Road, SE1 7DG

Matilda Clover (aka Phillips), 27, lived in two rooms on the second floor here with her young child. She was "living a loose life" and tended to drink heavily. On the evening of October 20, 1891 she was seen returning home with a tall man wearing a silk top hat who was likely to be Dr Thomas Neill Cream.

She popped out to get two beers and then spent another hour with him before he left. At 3am she woke, screaming in pain. She died at 9am on October 21, 1891. The doctor assumed it was due to excessive drinking and the police weren't informed. Her body was exhumed on May 5, 1892 once the connection had been made with other murders, and the post-mortem showed strychnine poisoning.

Monument Pub, 135 Union Street, Southwark SE1 0FA

Returning to London from Hertfordshire, George Chapman and his wife Bessie took over the license of the Monument Pub in March 1900. In December of that year, she started suffering with abdominal pains, vomiting and diarrhoea. She first saw a doctor on January 1, 1901. She died here on February 13, 1901.

In August 1901 Chapman advertised for a barmaid and Maud Eliza Marsh, aged 19, applied. They 'married' in October 1901.

On October 25, the Monument caught fire, and although Chapman didn't gain financially many thought he had torched the place.

It was never rebuilt and was replaced with a modern office building.

The Crown, 213 Borough High Street, SE1 1JA

From November 11, 1901 George Chapman took over The Crown, with Maud Eliza Marsh by his side.

She died here on October 22, 1902 following a long illness where the Marsh family doctor from Croydon thought she had been poisoned with arsenic.

The doctor was suspicious and insisted on carrying out a post-mortem. Traces of arsenic were found in her stomach as well as antimony.

On October 25, 1902, the police went to the Crown to speak to George Chapman about poisoning his wife. He was arrested later that day. Now a derelict building but if you look up you can still see the crown moulding.

The Crown, 213 Borough High Street, SE1 1JA

West

3-4 Archer Street, Piccadilly, W1D 7AP

Josephine Martin (known as French Fifi) had lived here since 1933. She was a Russian prostitute and was found by her maid on Monday November 4, 1935 dead on her bed. She had been strangled with her own silk stockings.

The murderer was never found.

47 Lexington Street, Soho, W1F 9AW

Marie Jeanet Cotton (née Cousins), a domestic servant lived in a second floor flat on Lexington Street. She lived with an Italian chef, Carlo Lanza, and his 15-year-old son. She returned to the flat from work on Thursday April 16, 1935 at 1pm and spoke with a neighbour at 5pm.

At 9pm her body was discovered. She had been strangled with a silk stocking and the coroner thought death was about 6:30pm. Her murderer was never found but likely to be the same person who killed Josephine Martin at Archer Street.

66 Old Compton Street, W1D 4UH

Leah Smith (aka Hinds) was in a relationship with Stanley King who did conjuring tricks for a living. When he found out she was a prostitute he wanted her to give it up. By May 1936 they were living in a second floor flat here at Old Compton Street. She was found on May 9, 1936 by King when he finished his night shift.

She had been strangled with a thin wire and beaten with a flat iron. An unusual fingerprint had been found on the mantelpiece, so the police sliced off the corner of the wood and took it to the police station.

This was another of the Soho serial killer's victims although he was never identified.

Blue Lagoon, 50 Carnaby Street, W1F 9QF

Margaret Cook was killed outside the Blue Lagoon on Carnaby Street by a .25 bullet from a German automatic pistol on November 9, 1946. She had been in a borstal, was well-known to the police in the area and was working as a prostitute.

In 2015, a 91-year-old man confessed to the previously-unsolved murder and it is thought to be the longest period of time between a crime and a confession.

The unnamed man, who now lives in Canada, was apparently prompted to admit the crime following a cancer diagnosis.

Metropolitan Police detectives flew out to interview him in his care home, and showed him pictures of 12 women, including Cook, and he successfully picked out his victim from the selection.

He said that he shot her with a WW2 Russian-made pistol after she cheated him out of money.

Newspaper reports from 1946, suggested her killer had been trying to take money from her. They also described a police chase of a man in a pork pie hat and Burberry-style raincoat in his mid to late twenties. The pursuit was unsuccessful, however, as the suspect vanished into the crowds.

He claims that five years later, he moved to the eastern Canadian province of Ontario, where he eventually became a citizen.

Today the nightclub is Nobody's Child.

Montagu Place (close to Gloucester Place), Marylebone, W1H 2ES

February 9, 1942 at about 8am the body of Evelyn Margaret Hamilton was found in a brick air-raid shelter on this street.

She'd been strangled. There was no sign of a struggle and no one saw anything.

RAF cadet pilot Frederick Gordon Cummins was charged in 1942 for a series of murders including this one.

Montagu Square, W1H 2LB
On April 7, 1823, John (aka Joseph) Mortland murdered poet Sir Warwick Bampfylde in Montagu Square. He then killed himself.

Mortland had been a servant working for Bampfylde and was jealous as his wife still worked there and he believed the 70-year-old Bampfylde was having an affair with her.

The bullet had got stuck in Bampfylde's ribs, but he died two weeks later of gangrene as some fabric from his braces had entered the wound.

Mortland was buried at a crossroads which is now a small triangle of unconsecrated ground opposite Lord's Cricket Ground with a stake through his heart. Suicide was considered illegal and it was thought they would return hence they were staked to the grave and buried at a crossroads. His was the last crossroads burial for this reason.

J.S. Jays Jewellers, 73-75 Charlotte Street, W1T 4PL
On April 28, 1947 three masked men Charles Jenkins, 23, Christopher Geraghty, 20, and Terence Rolt, 17, attempted to rob the jewellers which once stood on this site. The current building is modern.

A shot was fired in the shop, and the assistant manager raised the alarm for the police. The gunmen fled the shop only to find their getaway car was blocked by a lorry. They ran towards Tottenham Court Road, where Alec de Antiquis drove his motorcycle in their path to block their escape. Chris Geraghty shot him in the head.

It took three weeks to find the gunmen, all based on Charles Jenkins leaving his jacket at the scene. Both Geraghty and Jenkins were arrested and charged with murder.

9/10 Gosfield Street, W1W 6HD
Margaret Florence Campbell Lowe lived on Gosfield Street whilst she was working as a prostitute. She picked up clients on Charing Cross Road, Oxford Street and Piccadilly. She was known by the other girls as 'The Lady' or 'The Pearl' as she was well-spoken.

She was found in her Gosfield Street flat on Friday February 13, 1942, after her friends and daughter hadn't seen her for two days. She had been strangled and her body mutilated after death.

She was another victim of RAF cadet pilot Gordon Frederick Cummins.

187 Sussex Gardens, Tyburnia, W2 2RH
The body of Doris Elizabeth Joaunnet was found in the ground floor flat of this building. She had been strangled and stabbed on the same day as Margaret Lowe (Friday February 13, 1942).

Doris had come to London from the North East of England and was working as a prostitute. However, she did not need to live this lifestyle as she had a wealthy husband and an income.

Doris and her husband had had dinner together on the night of February 12, and they walked to Paddington station together as she saw him off to work. She then solicited on Sussex Gardens rather than heading home.

She was another victim of RAF cadet pilot Gordon Frederick Cummins.

Duke's Meadow, Duke's Meadow Car Park, Chiswick, W4 2SH

The body of Elizabeth Figg was found on June 17, 1959 on Duke's Meadow and is thought to have been the first victim of Jack the Stripper. She had been a prostitute in Bayswater and had been strangled.

Corney Reach (access to underside of Barnes Bridge via Thames Tradesmen's Rowing Club) Chiswick, W4 2SH

Irene Lockwood (aka Sandra Russell) was found dead on April 8, 1964 under Barnes Bridge, near Duke's Meadows, not far from where Hannah Tailford had been found. She had been in the river for approximately three days, and she was four months pregnant at the time of her murder.

It was only with the discovery of Lockwood that the police realized a serial killer was at large. The press nicknamed him Jack the Stripper.

48 Berrymede Road, Chiswick, W4 5JD

Scottish-born Mary Theresa Fleming (aka Mary Theresa Turner) was found dead on July 14, 1964 on the drive of this house.

Her false teeth were missing, and paint spots were also found on the body. Many neighbours had also heard a car reversing down the street just before the body was discovered. She was unlikely to have been killed here, but instead was dumped by Jack the Stripper.

London Corinthian Sailing Club, (below Linden House), Hammersmith, W6 9TA

On Sunday February 2, 1964 George and Douglas Capon discovered Hannah Tailford's body under the pontoon here. Her body had been in the water for a couple of days before discovery. She had been strangled, and several of her teeth were missing and was another of Jack the Stripper's victims.

Kensington Central Library, Kensington, W8 7RX

Another Scot, Frances Brown (aka Margaret McGowen, Frances Quin, and Alice Sutherland), was a prostitute and was last seen alive on October 23, 1964 by a colleague who saw her get into a client's car. The car was identified as a grey Ford Zephyr.

On November 25, her body was found in a car park on Hornton Street, which is now where Kensington Library is located. She had been strangled by Jack the Stripper.

Heron Trading Estate, 14 Alliance Court, Alliance Road, W3 0RB

Irish immigrant Bridget "Bridie" O'Hara was found dead on February 16, 1965 near a storage shed behind the Heron Trading Estate.

She had been missing since January 11. There were flecks of industrial paint on the body which were traced to an electrical transformer near where she was discovered.

This was also the site where the murder suspect, Mungo Ireland worked as a security guard.

[59] Braybrook Street, W12 0AS

A Vanguard car entered Braybook Street and attracted the attention of a police car who flagged them down.

DC Wombwell and DS Head approached the driver's window. Head asked the driver John Edward Witney for his road fund license, driver's license and insurance. Head then walked around the car, inspecting it, as Wombwell bent down to speak to the driver again.

Passenger, Harry Roberts then shot him in the eye. As Head fled back to the police car, John Duddy and Roberts jumped out the car, and Roberts shot Head in the back. Duddy then shot at Fox in the driver's seat of the police car hitting him in the head.

71a Elsham Road, West Kensington, W14 8HD

65-year-old Theodora Jessie Greenhill, a widow, advertised in the autumn of 1941 for a lodger through a local estate agent.

On October 14, 1941 Harold Trevor, visited her and paid the deposit on the flat. As she was writing the receipt he hit her on the head with a beer bottle, knocking her out. He then strangled her and rifled through the flat looking for things to steal.

Trevor's big mistake was giving his real name to Mrs Greenhill, so when the police arrived the unfinished receipt bore the killer's name. Trevor was known to the police, as in the previous 40 years he had only been out of prison for eleven months.

Leicester Square, WC2H 7LU

On December 9, 1692 the 4th Baron Mohun, Charles Mohun, along with Richard Hill ambushed actor William Mountfort in Leicester Square and stabbed him, killing him.

Leicester Square at the time was known as Leicester Fields and was a residential area, which had been constructed in 1670. The square in the middle is likely to be on the original footprint.

23 Cecil Court, WC2N 4EZ

On March 2, 1961, a scruffy young man came into Louis Meier's Antique shop at 23 Cecil Court and asked about a dress sword and ornamental daggers that were for sale.

The next day, an apprentice sign maker came into the shop to buy a billiards cue. He saw what he thought was a dummy in the back room on the floor and ended up leaving the shop without investigating.

When Mr Meier returned he found his assistant Elsie May Batten had been murdered with an ivory-handled dagger. Following descriptions of the youth given by Mr Meier and the owner of a local gun shop where the same youth had tried to sell a stolen sword from Mr Meier's store, Edwin Bush a 21-year-old Indian was arrested.

Savoy Hotel, Strand, WC2R 0EZ

On July 10, 1923 the night porter heard three gunshots, and saw a young woman, Madame Marguerite Fahmy, throw a gun to the floor in front of a man, her Egyptian husband Prince Ali Fahmy Bey slumped in the corner. She was heard to say repeatedly in French 'What have I done, my dear?'

Throughout their stay there had been violent public rows and evidence of physical violence by both husband and wife.

Abbey Court Hotel (Was Pembridge Court Hotel), Pembridge Gardens, Notting Hill, W2 4DU

June 21, 1946, the body of a woman, Margery Gardner, was found on the bed, murdered. She had been mutilated and bound.

She had been seen arriving at the hotel at around midnight with Neville Heath.

REFERENCES

Arnold, C., 2007: *Necropolis: London and its Dead.* Simon & Schuster UK. London.

Davies, C., 2021: *Queens of the Underworld: A Journey into the Lives of Female Crooks.* The History Press. Cheltenham.

Faulkner, B., 2020: *London Crime.* BSA Publishing. London.

Gamman, L., 2012: *Gone Shopping. The Story of Shirley Pitts – Queen of Thieves.* Bloomsbury Reader. London.

McDonald, B., 2015: *Alice Diamond and The Forty Elephants.* Milo Books Ltd. London.

St Clair, L. & Winfield, P. 1993: *Miss Whiplash: My Sensational Life Story.* Pan books. London.

Wise, S., 2004: *The Italian Boy: Murder and Grave-Robbery in 1830s London.* Pimlico Books. London.

Oates, Jonathan, 2022: *London Serial Killers.* Pen & Sword. Barnsley.

Thompson., L., 2018: *A Different Class of Murder: The Story of Lord Lucan.* Apollo. New York.

Clarkson, W., 2012: *The Curse of Brink's-Mat: Twenty Five Years of Murder and Mayhem.* Quercus. London.

Levi, J., 2017: *Hatton Garden: The Inside Story of Britain's Most Notorious Heist.* Blink Publishing. London.

Bondeson, J., 2015: *Murder Houses in London.* Amberley. London.

ine
INDEX

Crime Index

4th Baron Mohun (1692) 56
Acid Bath Murders (1945-9) 127
Baker Street Robbery (1971) 43
Blackout Ripper (1942) 122
Bobbed-Hair Bandit (1926-1940) 31
Brides in the Bath (1912-1914) 115
Brink's-Mat Robbery (1983) 46
Burlington Arcade Smash and Grab (1964) 43
Carnaby Street Shooting (1946) 81
Casserley Murder (1938) 77
Castle Street Murder (1878) 66
Catherine Hayes (1726) 58
Catherine Walters (1860s) 22
Cato Street Conspiracy (1820) 15
Caxton Hall Murder (1940) 78
Cecil Court Murder (1961) 86
Charing Cross Trunk Murder (1927) 76
Charlotte Street Robbery (1947) 82
Covent Garden Murder (1948) 84
Criminal Sculptor (1886) 138
Deptford Poisonings (1885-89) 98
Dr Crippen (1910) 71
Eastcastle Street Robbery (1952) 40
Elizabeth McLindon (1946) 79
Elsham Road Murder (1941) 79
Eltham Common Murder (1918) 72
Emily Dimmock (1907) 70
Finborough Road Murder (1922) 72
Forty Thieves (1890s-1950s) 28
George Chapman (1897-1903) 114
Goldman Sachs Theft (2004) 53
Graff Diamonds Robbery (2009) 49

Hatton Garden Heist (2015) 49
Hawley Crescent Murder (1933) 77
Highway Robbery 19
Italian Boy (The) (1831) 61
Jack the Ripper (1888) 100
Jack the Stripper (1963-5) 132
John Mortland (1823) 61
Kray Twins (1966) 87
Lambeth Poisonings (1891-92) 110
Lilian Goldstein (1926-1940) 31
Lord Lucan (1974) 93
Margery Gardner (1946) 82
Massacre of Braybrook Street (1966) 90
Millennium Dome Raid (2000) 48
Miss Whiplash (1980s) 23
Noreen Harbord (1946) 17
Ratcliff Highway Murders (1811) 59
Ripper of Rillington Place (1953) 130
Ruth Ellis (1955) 84
Savoy Murder (1923) 75
Security Express Robbery (1983) 46
Shirley Pitts (1950s) 35
Siege of Muswell Hill (1965) 139
Smuggling 17
Soho Serial Killings (1935-36) 120
Temple Murder (1733) 58
Treason 13
Turner Street Murder (1896) 68
Vagrancy (1820s) 136
Vandalism 136
Westminster Abbey Robbery (1303) 26
Whitechapel Murders (1888) 100
Whitechapel Road Murder (1874) 64
Zoe Progl (1960) 41

Areas of London (By postcode)

E1 7, 8, 9, 55, 59, 60, 63, 64, 65, 68, 69, 70, 87, 100, 101, 103, 104, 105, 106, 107, 108, 109, 156, 160, 163, 169, 177, 178, 179

E11 114

E12 110, 164

E13 9, 165

E14 17, 170,

E17 9, 110, 165

E1W 140, 170

E2 55, 88, 163, 169

E3 64, 162

E4 9, 88, 164

E6 8, 66, 67, 106, 116, 179

E7 109, 164

EC1 149, 170

EC1A 142, 157, 160

EC1M 9, 47, 52, 170, 171

EC1N 7, 49, 50, 51

EC1V 106, 114, 136

EC1Y 88, 104, 179

EC2A 46, 172

EC2E 84, 179

EC2V 13, 160

EC3A 104, 179

EC3N 9, 28, 104, 142, 143, 144, 149, 156

EC4A 53, 145

EC4M 9, 16, 28, 31, 34, 46, 47, 48, 58, 59, 63, 66, 71, 72, 75, 76, 78, 79, 80, 81, 82, 85, 87, 88, 93, 100, 112, 115, 118, 126, 131, 133, 138, 150, 157

EC4Y 53, 58, 59, 179

HA9 34,

HP7 86

N1 50, 52

N10 139

N14 52, 168

N16 88, 162

N19 116, 118, 176

N2 118, 163

N6 116, 162

N7 41, 71, 76, 79, 82, 84, 85, 87, 132, 150

N9 52, 163

NW1 7, 8, 39, 43, 44, 45, 49, 70, 77, 90, 91, 126, 168, 176

NW10 23, 34, 152

NW3 85

NW577, 118, 152,

NW8 111, 127

SE1 7, 8, 9, 22, 28, 39, 55, 62, 64, 89, 111, 112, 115, 137, 138, 148, 156, 161, 166, 183

SE10 48

SE11 9, 93, 148

SE15 162

SE16 88, 161

SE18 72, 116

SE27 133, 162

SE28 49, 52, 151

SE4 172

SE8 98, 161

SE9 72

SW10 9, 72, 162, 181, 182

SW11 130, 132

SW15 19, 180

SW17 40, 97, 111, 167

SW18 8, 80, 115, 127, 129, 130, 151

SW19 78

SW1A 9, 57, 137, 152, 153, 154, 172

SW1H 8, 78, 79, 180

SW1P7, 9, 13, 14, 26, 58, 76, 161, 180

SW1V 42

SW1W 8, 80, 94, 95, 97, 172, 180
SW1X 7, 8, 29, 36, 82, 172
SW1Y 111
SW2 9, 75, 118, 126, 132, 151
SW20 77, 129, 182
SW3 76, 84
SW5 7, 23, 25
SW6 129
SW7 7, 9, 17, 18, 127, 128, 129, 181
SW9 9, 116, 117
TW4 147
TW8 133
TW9 132
UB7 47, 155
W10 130, 162
W11 129, 130, 133, 134, 154, 175
W12 8, 9, 90, 91, 92, 93, 118, 119, 135, 154, 160, 175, 187
W14 79, 187
W1A 7, 36, 37, 38
W1B 7, 23, 29, 30, 33, 34, 61, 125
W1C 7, 13, 20, 54, 146
W1D 30, 35, 61, 72, 73, 74, 120, 121, 122, 123, 127, 183, 184
W1F 8, 30, 81, 120, 183, 184

W1H 7, 8, 9, 15, 23, 58, 61, 122, 123, 157, 158, 173, 184, 185
W1J 7, 8, 9, 21, 23, 39, 43, 57, 95, 96, 124, 173
W1K 7, 8, 22, 23, 24, 32, 33, 85
W1T 7, 8, 40, 41, 72, 82, 83, 112, 113, 174, 185
W1U 7, 8, 9, 35, 36, 102, 122, 123, 174
W1W 9, 125, 185
W2 9, 29, 47, 82, 124, 126, 133, 159, 188
W4 133, 47, 154, 186, 132
W6 76, 132, 134, 186
W8 9, 129, 134, 174, 175, 186
W9 91
WC1H 7, 47, 48
WC1N 154
WC1R 136
WC2A 9, 146
WC2B 9, 147
WC2E 7, 20, 42, 63, 87, 97, 112, 118, 126, 155, 156, 160
WC2H 7, 9, 23, 56, 141, 159, 187
WC2N 7, 8, 9, 19, 74, 76, 86, 116, 155
WC2R 8, 14, 25, 61, 75

Site Index

40 Elephants Cocktail Bar (The), 3-5 Great Scotland Yard, SW1A 2HN 7, 137, 172

43 Club, 43 Gerrard Street, W1D 5QQ 30

Abbey Court Hotel (Was Pembridge Court Hotel), Pembridge Gardens, Notting Hill, W2 4DU 82, 188

Ace Corner, North Circular Road, NW10 7UD 23

Additional Ground in Drury Lane (The) (Now Drury Lane Gardens), 57 Drury Lane, WC2B 5SN 9, 147, 162

Agar Grove (29) (was St Paul's Road), NW1 9UG 70, 176

Alderney Road Cemetery, Stepney, E1 4EG 55, 163

Aldgate High Street (29), EC3N 1DL 104

Almeric Road, Battersea (6), SW11 1HL 130

Archer Street (3-4), Piccadilly, W1D 7AP 9, 120, 121, 183

Archway Road (31), N19 3TU 116

Astor Club, 57 Berkeley Square, W1J 6ER 39

Augustus Street, NW1 3TJ 40

Barnes Borough Council Household Refuse Disposal Site, Townmead Road, TW9 4EL 132

Basement Flat, 10 Fernhead Road, Maida Vale, W9 3ET 91

Belmarsh Prison, Western Way, SE28 0EB 52, 151

Berry Bros. & Rudd, 3 St James's Street, SW1A 1EG 17

Berrymede Road (48), Chiswick, W4 5JD 134, 186

Bismarck Road (14) (Waterlow Road), Highgate, N19 5NH 118, 176

Bletsoe Walk (14), Islington, N1 7HZ 52

Blind Beggar Pub, 337 Whitechapel Road, E1 1BU 8, 87, 169, 177

Blue Lagoon, 50 Carnaby Street, W1F 9QF 8, 81, 184

Boston Manor Road (199), off Swyncombe Avenue, Brentford, TW8 9LE 133

Bow Street Magistrates' Court, 4 Bow Street WC2E 7AH 42, 63, 87, 97, 118, 155

Bow Street Police Museum, 28 Bow Street, WC2E 7AW 156

Braithwaite House (43), St Luke's, EC1Y 8NE 88

Braybrook Street (59), W12 0AS 8, 91, 92

Brick Lane (1), E1 7SA 8, 100, 101

Brixton Prison, Jebb Avenue, Brixton Hill, SW2 5XF 9, 75, 132, 161

Brixton Road (369), SW9 7DE 9, 116

Brockley Barge (was The Breakspeare Arms), 184 Brockley Road, SE4 2RR 99, 172

Brockley Cemetery, 113 Brockley Grove, SE4 1DZ 99, 167

Bucknall Street (2), WC2H 8LA 71

Burlington Arcade (41), 51 Piccadilly, W1J 0QJ 7, 21, 43

Carpenters Arms (The), 73 Cheshire Street, Bethnal Green, E2 6EG 88, 169

Carroll's Club, 58 Duke Street, Mayfair, W1K 6JW 8, 85

Cartier, 40-41 Old Bond Street, W1S 4QR 7, 31

Castle Farringdon (The), 34-35 Cowcross Street, EC1M 6DB 9, 52, 170, 171

Castle Pub (The) (was Warwick Castle Pub), 225 Portobello Road, W11 1LU 134, 175

Castle Pub, 54 Pentonville Road, N1 9HF 50, 168

Catchpole and Williams, 510 Oxford Street, W1K 7JA 7, 32, 33

Cato Street (1a), W1H 5HG 7, 15

Caxton Hall, 8-10 Caxton Street, SW1H 0AQ 8, 78, 180

Cecil Court (23), WC2N 4EZ 8, 86, 187

Chamber Street (45), E1 8BL 107, 179

Charing Cross Station, Strand, WC2N 5HF 76

Chester Square (45), SW1W 9EA 80, 180

Chester Square (51), SW1W 9EA 8, 97

Chingford Mount Cemetery, 121 Old Church Road, E4 6ST 9, 88, 164

Chiswick Police Station, 209-211 Chiswick High Road, W4 2DU 47, 154

Church Lane (7), Bushwood, E11 1HG 114

City of London Cemetery, Aldersbrook Road, E12 5DQ 110, 164

Clermont Club, 44 Berkeley Square, W1J 5AR 8, 95, 96

Coram's Fields, 93 Guilford Street, WC1N 1DN 154

Corner of Cable Street and Cannon Street Road, E1 0BL 59

Corney Reach (access to underside of Barnes Bridge via Thames Tradesmen's Rowing Club), Chiswick, W4 2SH 133, 186

Cowcross Street, EC1M 6BY 47

Creak Street (5), Deptford, SE8 3BT 100

Crossbones Cemetery, Union Street, SE1 1SD 22, 55, 166

Crown (The), 213 Borough High Street, SE1 1JA 9, 115, 183

Crown and Dolphin Pub, 56 Cannon Street Road, E1 0BL 7, 60

Culpeper Pub (was Princess Alice), 40 Commercial Street, E1 6TB 8, 108, 109, 169

Cumberland Hotel, 1 Great Cumberland Place, W1H 7DL 23

Curzon Street (39), W1J 7TZ 23

Dartmouth Park Road (43), Highgate, NW5 1SU 77

Dawes Road (16), Fulham, SW6 7EN 129

Dean Street (72), W1D 3SG 61

Debenhams, 27-37 Wigmore Street, W1U 1PN 7, 35, 36

Delhi Grill, 21 Chapel Market, N1 9EZ 52

Denbigh Road (16), Notting Hill, W11 2SN 133

Dorset Street (35), W1U 6QR 8, 103, 174

Duke Street (8), St James's, SW1Y 6BL 111

Duke's Meadow, Duke's Meadow Car Park, Chiswick, W4 2SH 132, 186

Eardley Crescent (58), SW5 9JZ 7, 23, 25

East Acton Station, W12 0BP 90

East Finchley Cemetery, 122 East End Road, N2 0RZ 118, 163

East London Cemetery, Grange Road, E13 0HB 9, 109, 165

Eastcastle Street, W1T 3QP 7, 40, 41

Eaton Row (5), SW1W 0JA 8, 95

Edmonton Cemetery, Church Street, N9 9HP 52, 163

Elizabeth Street (72a), SW1W 9PD 8, 95

Elkington's, 22 Regent Street, St James's, W1B 5RL 7, 33, 34

Elsham Road (71a), West Kensington, W14 8HD 8, 79, 187

Eltham Common (near Eltham Woolwich Road), SE9 6UA 72

Embassy Club, 7 Old Bond Street, W1S 4PN 7, 37, 39

Euston Station, Greater, Euston Road, NW1 2RT 39

Evering Road (97), Stoke Newington, N16 7SJ 88, 176

Finborough Road (13a), SW10 9DF 9, 72, 181, 182

Fireworks Factory (The) (was Woolwich Arsenal Works), 11 No 1 Street, Royal Arsenal, SE18 6HD 72

Fortnum and Mason, 181 Piccadilly, St James's, W1A 1ER 7, 37, 38

Friendly Street, Deptford, SE8 4DT 98

Frith Street (47), W1D 4HT 127

Gap Road Cemetery, Gap Road, SW19 8JA 78

Globe Fields, Whitechapel (Now Globe Road Memorial Gardens), E2 0LE 55

Globe Tavern, 8 Bedale Street, SE1 9AL 9, 137, 138

Gloucester Crescent (1), Regent's Park, NW1 7DS 126, 176

Gloucester Place (76), W1U 6DQ 9, 122, 123

Gloucester Road (79), SW7 5BW 9, 127, 129

Goat Tavern, 3A Kensington High Street, W8 5NP 9, 129, 174, 175

Graff Diamonds, 6-7 New Bond Street, W1S 3SJ 49

Grand Drive (9), Raynes Park, SW20 0JB 129

Grand Hotel, Northumberland Avenue, WC2N 5BY 8, 74

Gun Tavern, Docklands, 27 Coldharbour, E14 9NS 17, 170

Guy's Hospital, Great Maze Pond, SE1 9RT 7, 61, 62, 115

Happy Days Chip Shop, 44/46 Goulston Street, E1 7TP 107

Harrington Gardens (61), SW7 4JZ 7, 17, 18

Harrods, 87-135 Brompton Road, SW1X 7XL 7, 29, 36

Harvey Nichols, 109-125 Knightsbridge, SW1X 7RJ 7, 35

Hawley Crescent (30), NW1 8QR 77, 176

Heathrow International Trading Estate, Unit 7, Green Lane, Hounslow, TW4 6HB 47

Hen & Chickens, 54 Borough High Street, SE1 1XL 8, 64

Henriques Street (was Dutfield's Yard, off Berner Street), E1 1NT 103, 177

Heron Trading Estate, 14 Alliance Court, Alliance Road, W3 0RB 134, 187

Hewson Manufacturing Company, Newman Passage, W1T 1EG 72

Hilton, 22 Park Lane, W1K 1BE 7, 23, 24

Holloway Prison, Parkhurst Road, N7 0NU 41, 85, 150

Holy Sepulchre Church, Holborn Viaduct, EC1A 2DQ 157, 160

Hounslow Heath, Hanworth Road, Hounslow TW4 5LJ 147

House of Lords, Houses of Parliament, Parliament Square, SW1A 0PW 57

Hyde Park, W1J 7NT 57

Islington Local History Centre, Patrick Coman House, 245 Skinner Street, EC1V 4NE 136

J.S. Jays Jewellers, 73-75 Charlotte Street, W1T 4PL 8, 82, 185

Jack the Ripper Museum, 12 Cable Street, E1 8JJ 9, 156

Johanna Street (35), SE1 7RG 31

Kennington Common, Kennington Park Road, SE11 4PP 9, 148

Kensington Central Library, Kensington, W8 7RX 134, 186

Kentish Town Police Station, 10-12A Holmes Road, NW5 3AE 77, 118, 152

King's College School of Anatomy, Strand, WC2R 2LS 61

Ladbroke Square (22), (Anglo Czech Welfare Association), W11 3NA 129

Lambeth Palace Road (103), SE1 7LG 112

Lambeth Road (27), SE1 7DG 111, 182

Lancaster Road (44), Notting Hill, W11 1QR 134

Le Sac, 189 Baker Street, NW1 6UY 7, 45

Leicester Square, WC2H 7LU 7, 23, 56

Lexington Street (47), Soho, W1F 9AW 120, 183

Liberty, Regent Street, Carnaby, W1B 5AH 7, 29, 30

Lilian Knowles House (was Providence Row Refuge), 50 Crispin Street, E1 6HQ 8, 106

Lincoln's Inn Fields, WC2A 3BP 9, 146

Lindesfarne Road (35), Wimbledon, SW20 0NW 77,182

Little Club (The), 37 Brompton Road, SW3 1DE 8, 84

Lloyd's Bank, 185 Baker Street, NW1 6XB 7, 43

London Corinthian Sailing Club, (below Linden House), Hammersmith, W6 9TA 132, 186

London Dungeon, Riverside Building, County Hall, Westminster Bridge Road, London SE1 7PB 156

London Hospital, Whitechapel Road, E1 1FR 8, 69, 70

Long Acre (126), EC2E 9PE 84, 179

Lower Belgrave Street (46), SW1W 0LN 8, 93, 94

Lower Richmond Road (2-4), SW15 1JN 130

Luton Airport, Airport Way, Luton LU2 9LY 46

Madison, 25 Hatton Garden, EC1N 8BQ 7, 50, 51

Magdala Public House, South Hill Park, NW3 2SB 85, 108, 177

Maison Lyons Corner House, 1 Marble Arch, W1H 7DX 9, 122, 123

Manor Park Cemetery, Sebert Road, Forest Gate, E7 0NP 109, 164

Marquis (The), (was The Hole in the Wall) 51-52 Chandos Place, WC2N 4HS 7, 19

Marylebone Magistrates' Court, 181 Marylebone Road, NW1 5BR 8, 49, 90, 91

Masons Arms, (now The Portman) 51 Upper Berkeley Street, W1H 7QW 9, 157, 158, 173

Millennium Dome, SE10 0BB 48

Mitre Court/Fetter Lane, EC4Y 1BN 59

Mitre Square, EC3A 5DE 104, 179

Monico Restaurant, 39-45 Shaftesbury Avenue, W1D 6LA 123

Montagu Place (close to Gloucester Place), Marylebone, W1H 2ES 123, 184

Montagu Square, W1H 2LB 61, 185

Monument Pub, 135 Union Street, Southwark, SE1 0FA 114, 182

Murray's "Cabaret" Club, 16-18 Beak Street, W1F 9RD 30

Nag's Head, 53 Kinnerton Street, Knightsbridge, SW1X 8ED 8, 82, 173

National Gallery, Trafalgar Square, WC2N 5DN 116

New Scotland Yard, Victoria Embankment, SW1A 2JL 9, 153, 154

Newgate Prison, Old Bailey, EC4M 7EH 142, 160, 157

Newington Green (was Horsemonger Lane Gaol), Harper Road, SE1 6PP 148

Norman Shaw Buildings, Victoria Embankment, SW1A 2JH 9, 153

Northumberland Arms Pub, 119 Tottenham Court Road, W1T 5AW 8, 112, 113, 174

Notting Hill Police Station, 99-101 Ladbroke Road, W11 3PL 130, 154

Odeon and Empire Cinemas, Leicester Square, WC2H 7LU 23

Old Bailey (was Newgate Prison), EC4M 7EH 9, 16, 28, 31, 34, 46, 57, 48, 58, 59, 63, 66, 71, 72, 75, 76, 78, 79, 80, 81, 82, 85, 87, 88, 93, 100, 112, 115, 118, 126, 131, 133, 142, 150, 157

Old Castle Street (was Castle Alley), Whitechapel, E6 1PP 8, 66, 67, 136, 179

Old Compton Street (66), W1D 4UH 122, 184

Old Eagle Pub, 251 Royal College Street, NW1 9LU 70, 168, 187

Onslow Court Hotel (The Kensington Hotel) 113 Queen's Gate, SW7 3LE 9, 127, 128

Orchard Road (16), Highgate, N6 5TR 116

Osborn Street, E1 6TD 100

Oxford Gardens (23), Notting Hill, W10 5UE 130

Oxford Gardens (35), Notting Hill, W10 5UF 130

Paddington Station, Praed Street, W2 1HU 47

Paris Jewels (was Hatton Garden Safety Deposit Ltd), 88-90 Hatton Garden, EC1N 8PN 49, 50

Parish Church of St Stephen and St Thomas 1 Coverdale Road, W12 8JJ 93, 160

Penguin Club, 27 Rupert Street, Soho, W1D 6DR 35

Pentonville Prison, Caledonian Road, N7 8TT 71, 76, 79, 82, 87, 132, 150

Peterborough Court, Fleet Street, EC4A 2BB 53

Pinchin Street, E1 1SA 107, 178

Plumbers Arms, 14 Lower Belgrave Street, SW1W 0LN 8, 94, 95, 172

Prince Edward Theatre (was Palace Theatre), Old Compton Street, W1D 4HS 122

Prince of Wales, 20 Bartholomew Square, Finsbury, EC1V 3QT 114

Punch Bowl Pub, 41 Farm Street, W1J 5RP 9, 124, 173

Quadrant Arcade, Regent Street, W1B 5RL 61,

Queen's Head Pub, 74 Commercial Street, E1 6LY 8, 103, 104

Railway Arch (103), Tinworth Street, Vauxhall, SE11 5EQ 93

Red Lion Square (13), WC1R 4QH 136

Regent Palace Hotel, 36 Glasshouse Street, W1B 5DL 23

Richmond Court (10), Forty Avenue, Wembley, HA9 8LL 34

Richmond Road (14), Shepherd's Bush, W12 8LY 118

Ritz Cinema, 277 Neasden Lane, NW10 1QJ 34

Rochester Row (86), SW1P 1LJ 9, 76, 180

Rocket (The) (was Rising Sun), 120 Euston Road, NW1 2AL 70, 168

Roman Road (92), Bethnal Green, E6 3SR 116

Royal Court Hotel, 7-12 Sloane Square, SW1W 8EG 125

Royal National Hotel, 38-51 Bedford Way, London WC1H 0DG 7, 47

Sandringham Flats, 87 Charing Cross Road, WC2H 0BN 23

Savoy Hotel, Strand, WC2R 0EZ 8, 23, 75

Scotti's Snack Bar, 38 Clerkenwell Green, EC1R 0DU 52

Selfridges, 400 Oxford Street, W1A 1AB 7, 36, 37

Sheen's Burial Ground, 52-58 Commercial Road and 109-153 Back Church Lane, E1 1LP 8, 63, 163

Shepherd's Bush Police Station, 252 Uxbridge Road, W12 7JA 8, 90, 154

Shooters Hill, SE18 4LG 19

Shoreditch Town Hall, 380 Old Street, EC1V 9LT 106

Sidney Square (3), Mile End Road, E1 2EY 8, 65

Sindercombe Social Club (was Shepherd's Bush Hotel) 2 Goldhawk Road, W12 8QD 9, 135, 175

Smallest Police Station, Trafalgar Square, WC2N 5DN 9, 155

South Street (15), W1K 2XB 7, 22

Southern Belle (The) (was Greyhound Hotel), 175 & 177 Fulham Palace Road, W6 8QT 76

Southerton Road (16a), Hammersmith, W6 0PH 134

Southwark Crown Court, 1 English Grounds, SE1 2HU 53

Southwark Magistrates' Court, 1 English Grounds, SE1 2HU 53

Southwark Police Court, 211 Tooley Street, SE1 2JY 28

Southwick Street (29), nr Sussex Gardens, Tyburnia, W2 1JQ 9, 124

St Bartholomew's Hospital, West Smithfield, EC1A 7BE 141

St George-in-the-East Church, 14 Cannon St Road, E1 0BH 7, 59, 60, 160

St George the Martyr, Borough High Street, SE1 1JA 55, 161

St George's Hall, 5 Westminster Bridge Road, SE1 7XW 138

St George's Hospital, Blackshaw Road, SW17 0QT 97

St Giles High Street, WC2H 8AB 9, 159

St Giles-in-the-Fields Churchyard, St Giles High Street, WC2H 8LG 9, 141

St James's Close (27), Regent's Park, NW8 7LQ 127

St Margaret's Church, St Margaret Street, SW1P 3JX 7, 26, 58, 161

St Mary's Church, Church Street, Old Amersham, HP7 0DB 86, 161

St Mary's Church, Saint Marychurch Street, SE16 4NF 88, 161
St Mary-le-Bow Church, Cheapside, EC2V 6AU 13, 160
St Nicholas' Church, Deptford Green, SE8 3DQ 98
St Pancras Hospital, 4 Saint Pancras Way, Pancras Road, NW1 0PE 77
St Patrick's Roman Catholic Cemetery, Langthorne Road, E11 4HL 9, 110, 114, 165
St Paul's Church Bedford Street, WC2E 9ED 7, 20, 63, 160
St Thomas' Hospital, Westminster Bridge Road, SE1 7EH 39, 111
Stamford Street (118), Blackfriars, SE1 9NN 28, 112
Statue of Queen Anne, St Paul's Churchyard, EC4M 8AD 9, 138
Strand (229-230), Temple, WC2R 1BF 14, 25
Sussex Gardens (187), Tyburnia, W2 2RH 9, 125, 126, 186
Sydney Street, Chelsea, SW3 6PX 76

Talbot Road (34), W2 5LJ 133
Tanza Road (29), NW3 2UA 85
Tate Modern, Bankside, SE1 9TG 8, 88, 89
Temple Bar Memorial, EC4A 2LT 145
Temple, EC4Y 9DA 58, 179
Ten Bells Pub, 84 Commercial Street, E1 6QQ 104, 105, 169
Thames Police Court, 79 Aylward Street, Stepney Green, E1 0QH 69
The Fox, 28 Paul Street, Shoreditch, EC2A 4LB 46, 172
Thrawl Street, E1 6RT 101
Thurlby Road (37), West Norwood, SE27 0RN 133

Tooting Cemetery, Blackshaw Road, Tooting, SW17 0BY 111, 167
Tower Hill, EC3N 4DX 9, 144
Tower of London, EC3N 4AB 9, 28, 142, 143, 149
Town of Ramsgate Pub (was Execution Dock), 62 Wapping High Street, E1W 2PL 140, 170
Townshend Road (44), St John's Wood, NW8 6LE 111
Tredegar Square (40), Bow, E3 5AE 64,
Trinity Square Gardens, Tower Hill, EC3N 4DX 9, 144
Turner Street (31), E1 2AS 8, 68, 178
Tyburn (Marble Arch), W1C 1LX 7, 11, 13, 20, 54, 58, 146, 157, 159

Uxbridge Road (60), Shepherd's Bush, W12 8LP 9, 118, 119

Viaduct Tavern, 126 Newgate Street, EC1 7AA 149, 157, 170

Walthamstow (St Patrick's) Roman Catholic Cemetery, Queen's Road, E17 8QP 9, 10, 114, 165
Wandsworth Prison, Heathfield, Road, SW18 3HU 8, 80, 115, 127, 129, 130, 151
Wardour Street (21), W1D 6PN 74
Wardour Street (27), W1D 6PN 74,
Warriner Street (27), Battersea, SW11 4EA 132
Warwick Square, Pimlico, SW1V 2AA 42
Wembley Park Drive (58), HA9 8HB 34
West Drayton Police Station, Station Road, West Drayton, Uxbridge, UB7 7JQ 47, 155

Westminster Abbey, Dean's Yard, SW1P 3PA 7, 14, 26

Westminster Hall, 3 St Margaret Street, SW1P 3JX 7, 13, 14

Westminster Magistrates' Court, 181 Marylebone Road, NW1 5BR 49

White House (The), 51 New Bond Street, W1S 1BJ 7, 33

Whitechapel Road (215), E1 1DE 8, 64, 65, 178

Whitechapel Road (84), E1 1DT 64,

Whitehall Place (4), SW1A 2EG 9, 152

Whiteley's, 149 Queensway, W2 4YN 29

Whites Row (8) (was Spitalfields Chambers), E1 7NF 8, 109

Willesden Police Station, 96 High Road, NW10 2PP 34, 152

Wimbledon Common, SW15 3SB 133

Windmill Pub, 214 Chiswick High Road, W4 1SD 133

Wizards and Wonders (was Lyons Corner House), 13 Coventry Street (corner of Rupert Street), W1D 7AG 8, 72, 73

Woodland Rise (65), Muswell Hill, N10 3UN 139

Woolwich Crown Court, 2 Belmarsh Way, SE28 0EY 49, 52

Wellington Street, SE18 6PW 116

Woolwich, 88 Fleet Street EC4Y 1DH 53

Working Lad's Institute, 283 Whitechapel Road, E1 1BY 8, 101, 102

Wymering Mansions, 181 Wymering Road, Maida Vale, W9 2NQ 91

Ye Frying Pan Pub, 16 Brick Lane, E1 6PU 8, 100, 101

Ye Olde Cherry Tree Pub, The Green, N14 6EN 52, 168